FOR ANOTHER FLOCK

FOR ANOTHER FLOCK

Daily Advent and Christmas Meditations
for Gay and Lesbian Christians

Jeffrey R. Lea

The Pilgrim Press
Cleveland

For Donnie

The Pilgrim Press, 700 Prospect Avenue, Cleveland, Ohio 44115-1100
thepilgrimpress.com
© 2005 Jeffrey R. Lea

Scriptural quotations from the New Revised Standard Version of the Bible are copyright
© 1989 by the Division of Christian Education of the National Council of Churches of Christ
in the U.S.A. and are used by permission. Changes have been made for inclusivity.

10 09 08 07 06 05   5 4 3 2 1

Library of Congress Cataloging-in-Publication Data

Lea, Jeffrey R., 1963–
    For another flock : daily Advent and Christmas meditations for gay and lesbian
Christians
   / Jeffrey R. Lea.
      p. cm.
    Includes bibliographical references.
    ISBN 0-8298-1612-7 (pbk. : alk. paper)
     1. Advent—Prayer-books and devotions—English.   2. Christmas—Prayer-books and
devotions—English.   3. Gays—Prayer-books and devotions—English.   4. Lesbians—Prayer-
books and devotions—English I. Title.

BV40.L43   2005
262'.33—dc22   2005045826

Contents

Preface

L IKE SO MUCH OF OUR STORY in society, the gay and lesbian experience of faith must be read between the lies used to straighten out our participation in religious history. Yet we have been around since before the love story of Jonathan and David was recorded in the Old Testament's First Book of Samuel.

In this book I seek to highlight some of the ancient and lively traditions of the Advent and Christmas seasons and explore them in a way that gay men and lesbian women are affirmed. I created these materials because I wanted Advent and Christmas resources that spoke to me out of my own experience. The material includes practices suitable for private meditation and activities intended for groups and families.

Each of the resources I've created is rooted in a biblical text. I know that the Bible has been used to silence, shame, negate, and abuse gay and lesbian persons, but as you begin to use this book it is important to be clear that the Holy Bible does not denigrate the experience of same-sex love, nor condemn us for the expressions of intimate love. In the history of biblical understanding, the idea that same-sex attraction is an "abomination" is relatively new. In addition, the use of the Old Testament to excoriate us is not a tradition inherited from the Jews. The relatively few passages in scripture that have been used to attack us have been misinterpreted, often deliberately. In the few instances where reference is made to same-sex sexual activity, it is done so in context with ritual and what is being attacked is the abuse of sex for religious purposes. At the same time, other practices are also condemned and the use of the word "abomination" is specifically related to practices that disparage the public practice of faith. Love between two men and two women, and its physical expression, are nowhere condemned in the Holy Bible. To the contrary, as noted above, in the love story of Jonathan and David same-sex love is extolled. For further exploration of this theme I recommend you read John Boswell's *Same Sex Unions in Pre-Modern Europe* and the Rev. Michael England's *The Bible and Homosexuality.*

Gay men and lesbian women attracted to the mystery of Christian faith can approach the Bible free of any misconceptions that the Bible attacks the foundation of who we are. On the contrary, in my experience Christian faith can provide a means of liberating our spirit so that with Mary, the Mother of God, we can accept the plan that God has in mind for our lives and say, "let it be done to me according to your word."

WHAT YOU'LL FIND HERE

I've created this book as both an individual and family/group guide to the practices of spiritual development available in Advent and have included daily, weekly, and seasonal activities. Each meditation in the book is based on the daily Bible readings for Advent and Christmas, as designated by the Revised Common Lectionary used by many Protestants and the Catholic Lectionary used by Roman Catholics. Lectionaries are lists of assigned Scripture texts for each Sunday of the church year as well as other feast days and holy days. The lectionary was established by the Catholic and Protestant churches so that each year Christians who follow a lectionary cycle can hear the full story of salvation and can all focus on specific scripture passages at the same time. There are three cycles of designated texts: Years A, B, and C. When Year C is complete the cycle begins again with Year A. "Reading Cycle for Advent and Christmas" (pp. 99–106) contains the complete list of readings for cycles A, B, and C.

In the section intended for group study (pp. 74–83) you will find materials that explore the Advent and Christmas themes of the second coming, penitential house cleaning, joyful expectation, and incarnate love. Invite a group of friends to gather in your home or hold the weekly meetings at your place of worship.

The version of Morning Prayer and Evening Prayer I've included is designed to incorporate the daily readings into your morning meditation and time for reflection on a Psalm both in the morning and the evening. Daily prayer and Bible readings can be done either individually or with others. As it is a common practice of the Advent season, a model of the seasonal practice of an "examination of conscience" is also included.

I have also provided practices designed around the Sundays of Advent that are geared toward developing the meaning of the season in the home and with a community of family or friends. Contemporary families reflect a wide variety of possible loving arrangements. The "gayby boom" includes male couples and female couples raising their own biological or adopted children. There are households that consist of a gay father and a lesbian mother raising children with their partners. There are two-person households and multi-person households. The diverse households are all valuable expressions of God's love and the family practices in this book are a way to deepen these relationships while exploring the Advent themes.

I am Roman Catholic and because I continue my journey in that faith tradition I have based the meditations in this book on the Roman Catholic *Lectionary for Mass* for Advent and Christmas. The scripture references come from the New Revised Standard Version (NRSV) of the Bible. I used a Bible published by Oxford University Press, which includes the Deutero-Canonical books and other elements of the Old Testament that are not included in the Protestant editions of the Bible. I have occasionally modified the portion of the biblical text I am bringing to your attention by using inclusive language for God or people.

HOW TO USE THIS BOOK
For Daily Meditation

(This 15 to 20 minutes each day can also be incorporated into the practice of morning or evening prayer.)

1. Read the Psalm at the beginning of each meditation. Notice what word or phrase stands out for you.

2. Read the Scripture texts listed for each meditation. Notice what word or phrase holds your attention.

3. Read the meditation.

4. Sit in silence. Recall which words or phrases from the Scripture drew your attention as you were reading. Listen for what the readings and

meditation are saying to you today. Answer these two questions: What are the texts and meditations saying to me today? What are the texts and meditation asking me to do or be today?

5. Pray the prayer at the end of the meditation. Feel free to add your own prayers as well.

As an aid to you I have repeated the directions for this suggested process in all the Sunday meditations. As the weeks go, if you find the process helpful, it will become second nature to you.

For Group Study—60 to 90 minutes each week

1. To prepare for each group study, ask the group members to read the Gospel and the commentary for that week. The Gospel indicated is the Sunday Gospel for that week.

2. When the participants have arrived and greeted one another, begin with a simple prayer and then read the Gospel aloud.

3. Discuss the questions that are provided. There may be more questions than you can address during each session. Select those that seem most important for the needs and interests of your group.

MY THANKS

There are far too many pioneers of gay and lesbian Christian faith for me to name or thank adequately. They range from St. John the Divine, to St. Anselm, to the courageous lesbian women and gay men of the last 100 years struggling to affirm publicly our identity as Christians as well. I would, however, be remiss if I failed to mention one important person. Without the constant love and support of my partner, Donnie Isaac, this book would not have been possible. My work reflects the emotional, spiritual, and material support that he gives me so generously.

PART ONE

A Short History of Advent and Christmas

THE LITURGICAL YEAR

THROUGHOUT THE LITURGICAL year the church celebrates the saving work of Jesus. The purpose is to commemorate the whole mystery of Christ, from his incarnation through Easter and Pentecost, until the expectation of his Second Coming on Christ the King Sunday. The center of the liturgical year is the Easter mystery in the passion and resurrection of Christ. Easter is the great Paschal feast of the year, but this mystery is also celebrated every Sunday.

There are three main divisions of the liturgical year. These are the Christmas Cycle (the mystery of the incarnation), the Easter Cycle (the mystery of the redemption), and Ordinary time (the season of the church). Advent is the season that opens the liturgical year. It derives its name from the Latin word *adventus*, which means "coming." It precedes and prepares us for the Christmas season that begins on December 24. The Advent season begins on the Sunday closest to the Feast of St. Andrew the Apostle (November 30). Depending upon the annual calendar, the season can last up to twenty-eight days if it begins as early as November 27, or it can be as short as twenty-one days if it begins as late as December 3.

ORIGINS OF ADVENT AND CHRISTMAS

The earliest feast celebrating the birth of Christ originated in the Eastern Church as Epiphany on January 6. It was also a baptismal feast and so, like Easter, it was felt that a penitential season was needed. The church in France and Spain was closely connected to Byzantium and so adopted the Eastern Church's celebration. The Council of Saragossa in Spain ordered penitential fasting before Epiphany in Spain in 330 AD and the Council of Macon ordered it for all of France in 581 AD.

The French Church's celebration highlighted an End Time attitude in the sixth century. This was due to the influence of Irish missionaries who had crossed over to the continent. The contemporary emphasis still maintains some element of the End Time character of Advent as it begins with a memorial to the Second Coming of Christ.

Epiphany was not a baptismal feast for the Church of Rome and so no penitential season was necessary prior to it, but that church did celebrate Christmas and needed a season of preparation. Christmas is believed to have grown out of a response to the establishment of an Imperial Roman feast first held in 274 AD as the birthday of the "unconquered sun god." By 336 AD the Roman Church was celebrating a feast of the birth of Christ as the "light of the world." The calendar of F.D. Filocalus in 354 AD indicates a Christmas celebration in Rome on December 25. During this period there were various attempts to fix the exact date of Jesus' birth. As there was a tradition of John the Baptist's birth falling on the summer equinox it was suggested that Jesus' birth would have been on the winter equinox. December 25 was the winter equinox in the Julian calendar.

By the end of the sixth century Pope Gregory I had fully developed the Advent season. Under his direction the liturgy was developed, lectionary readings assigned, and it was incorporated into the "Liturgy of the Hours." His "sacramentary" (book of rituals) included four Sunday Masses for this season. The emphasis of the Advent season in Rome was incarnational and did not focus on the End Time theme. Its focus was on the birth of Christ. When the Roman Advent season was introduced in France in the twelfth century the season was fully developed, although the End Time theme found in the French tradition was incorporated into it. Current practice emphasizes both the preparation for Christ's birth and the expectation of the Second Coming. However, the early Roman Church attitude is preeminent in that Advent is a period for joyous expectation.

THE THEME OF ADVENT

Advent celebrates the coming of Jesus in his birth, his earthly ministry, and his Second Coming. It is also a period of preparation and so shares some element of the penitential aspect of Lent. It is a time when we acknowledge what God has done for us through Jesus and what is going to be done for us in the final fulfillment of God's will. This creates a certain spiritual tension in the season between the joyfulness of the coming of Christ and the preparatory aspect of it, which involves the cleansing characteristic of penance. A good metaphor would be cleaning one's home in expectation of the arrival of houseguests.

This dynamic between joy and penance is played out most clearly in the Advent Bible readings. In the Sunday readings the focus begins with the Second Coming of Jesus, moves through the preparatory period of John the Baptist on the second and third Sundays, and concludes with the joy of the annunciation and Mary's visit to Elizabeth on the fourth Sunday. The weekday readings trace this development as well. During the first nine weekdays of Advent the Isaiah readings look forward to the coming messianic age. After the Thursday of the second week the readings focus on John the Baptist until December 17 when they shift to the description of the events leading to Christ's birth as found in Matthew and Luke.

ADVENT AND GAY AND LESBIAN CHRISTIANS

Are gay and lesbian people preparing for and waiting expectantly for something? Indeed, full acceptance into both church and society is an incarnation that we anxiously await. Advent, however, can help us see that the primary acceptance we await is within ourselves.

The Reign of God is always at hand, and, therefore saving grace is constantly available to us. It is not necessary for the world at large to acknowledge the legitimacy of our claim to be who we are, and to do so in the light of Christian faith. As Christian people we await the final affirmation that God's truth will proclaim. As gay and lesbian Christians that particular proclamation is an affirmation of who we are and an affirmation that we already enjoy the saving grace of Jesus Christ.

During Advent we can more fully explore the meaning of God's will in our lives as gay and lesbian Christians and how that will is worked out ultimately in the future, and incarnationally now. We can sweep out the cobwebs of self-doubt and decorate our house with joy and gratitude.

PART TWO

Daily Meditations for Advent and Christmas

INTRODUCTION

THE MEDITATIONS INCLUDED cover the maximum number of days possible in Advent and Christmas. Naturally, the number of days fluctuates based on the yearly calendar. In order to follow the cycle for each year you will need to consult the current calendar during week three of Advent to find on what day of the week December 17 falls. When December 17 arrives go directly to the dated meditations provided for December 17 through January 6. On Sunday of the week following December 17, use the Sunday reading for the fourth Sunday of Advent. You can consult "Reading Cycle for Advent and Christmas" (pp. 99–106) for more detailed instructions on using the lectionary calendar.

THE FIRST WEEK OF ADVENT: PROMISE AND FULFILLMENT
The First Sunday of Advent

PSALM

Read the Psalm twice, pausing for a few minutes between readings. Notice which word or phrase stands out for you.

> Restore us, O God;
> let your face shine,
> that we may be saved.
> (Ps 80:3)

SCRIPTURE

Read the appropriate texts depending on whether it is year A, B, or C. See "Reading Cycle for Advent and Christmas" (pp. 99–106). Notice what word or phrase holds your attention.

Catholic Lectionary	Revised Common Lectionary
Year A:	Year A:
Isa 2:1–5;	Isa 2:1–5;
Ps 122:1–9;	Ps 122;
Rom 13:11–14a;	Rom 13:11–14;
Mt 24:37–44	Mt 24:36–44
Year B:	Year B:
Isa 63:16b–17, 19b, 64:2b–7;	Isa 64:1–9;
Ps 80:2–3, 15–19;	Ps 80:1–7, 17–19;
1 Cor 1:3–9;	1 Cor 1:3–9;
Mk 13:33–37	Mk 13:24–37
Year C:	Year C:
Jer 33:14–16;	Jer 33:14–16;
Ps 25:4–5, 8–12, 14;	Ps 25:1–10;
1 Thess 3:12–4:2;	1 Thess 3:9–13;
Lk 21:25–28, 34–36	Lk 21:25–36

Meditation

Advent is a period of joyful expectation and preparation as we await the coming of Jesus. During this time, we are waiting for both his incarnation at Christmas and his Second Coming in the fulfillment of God's promise of love to us. As a gay person why should I celebrate a Christian mystery? What am I preparing for? Why should I wait for a promise that seems so often to be a condemnation of who I am? What does this Christian faith or practice offer to deepen the understanding of my gay experience?

The Book of Isaiah says that we are the clay; God is the potter (Isa 64:8). All of us are the work of God's hands. I am gay, not because of sin, but because God cast me on the wheel and spun me this way. I waited in the closet for a long time—too scared to admit that I was gay and angry that God had made me so different. I even tried to pretend that I was straight in a heterosexual marriage. But denial and dishonesty would not recast this clay. By lying to myself, to others and to God I became Isaiah's "one who is unclean" (Isa 64:6). When I came out of the closet I began to live the truth. I began to understand that being gay was my incarnated gift from God and I could celebrate who I am. Other gay and lesbian people I have known struggled with these same issues of faith and prepared the way for me, just as I now help to prepare the way for those coming after me. If I stay watchful over this gift of gay incarnation, then, as St. Paul says, I will receive the strength promised me to be irreproachable as I wait for the Day of our Lord (1 Cor 1:8).

So I have a good reason to await Christ's coming. I have good reason to prepare myself for it. And I have good reason to celebrate the creation of same-sex love in the incarnation of God's love.

SILENCE

Sit in silence. Recall what words or phrases from the Scripture drew your attention as you were reading. Listen for what the readings and meditation are saying to you today. Answer these two questions: What are the texts and meditations saying to me today? What are the texts and meditation asking me to do or be today?

PRAYER

Be with me while I wait, Lord,
and help me to prepare and celebrate the divine gift of love
you have given me.

Monday of the First Week of Advent

PSALM

I was glad when they said to me,
"Let us go to the House of the Lord!"
For the sake of my relatives and friends
I will say, "Peace be within you!"
(Ps 122:1, 8)

SCRIPTURE

Isaiah 2:1–5, Psalm 122:1–9, Matthew 8:5–11

Meditation

Isaiah tells of the time when warfare and strife between people will come to an end. The Christian message is that this promise is always imminent, "on earth as it is in heaven." Jesus shows us how this promise is always at hand, even in the most unexpected places, when a Roman centurion, a foreign military officer and a pagan occupier, manifests the promise through his words.

To believe this promise requires faith. Faith is also the action we take to realize the promise in our time. In Matthew, Jesus makes it clear that in the unusual, the strange, the marginalized the promise comes true. By experiencing the fundamental reality of same-sex love, I have faith that this promise is imminent. By loving my partner and proclaiming the truth openly I put my faith in action. While the promise of an end to strife and oppression is made manifest in my life, I await the ultimate fulfillment of it when in Christ there will be neither east nor west, neither top nor bottom.

Silence

Prayer

Lord, I am not worthy to receive you,
but you sent the word and I am healed.

Tuesday of the First Week of Advent

Psalm

May God's name endure forever,
God's fame continue as long as the sun.
May all nations be blessed in God;
may they pronounce God happy.
(Ps 72:17)

Scripture

Isaiah 11:1–10; Psalm 72:1, 7–8, 12–13, 17; Luke 10:21–24

MEDITATION

Today Isaiah foretells the messianic age, God's reign, and describes the unusual and unbelievable nature of that time. In Luke, Jesus again shows us that those times are these times when he says, "Blessed are the eyes that see what you see" (Luke 10:23).

And what do we see in our lifetime? On the one hand we see violence, oppression, division, and hate. On the other hand we see the coming together of previously unheard of combinations. Relationships that at one time would have been unbelievable at best, abominable at worst, are now a part of our own lives. The cow and the bear grazing together, a child at play with a snake! These are all signs of God's love made manifest.

I was raised in a world that said that it was wrong for the wolf to lie down with the lamb. When I saw a white man walking hand-in-hand with a black woman, to me the unbelievable had arrived. And when I saw two men living together in a mutually supportive love relationship, God demonstrated that the unbelievable is truth. The usual, the customary, the easy to do and believe is not the way. As Isaiah shows us, the unusual, the challenging, the radical is the sign of God's norm. And God's truth is always available for us to receive. We reach out in faith for the promise of an end to division and oppression and the Messiah is there.

SILENCE

PRAYER

Thank you, Jesus,
for having chosen to reveal your truth to us all.

Wednesday of the First Week of Advent

PSALM

You prepare a table before me
in the presence of my enemies;
you anoint my head with oil;
my cup overflows.
(Ps 23:5)

SCRIPTURE

Isaiah 25:6–10a; Psalm 23:1–6; Matthew 15:29–37

MEDITATION

The Messianic promise of a world turned upside down by God's vision continues to be revealed in Isaiah during this first week of Advent. In today's Gospel reading the promise is described as a great feast. Matthew describes a miraculous feast of abundance that Jesus prepared for the large crowd following him. Isaiah describes the ultimate fulfillment of God's promise and Jesus reveals how God's vision of enough for all is already imminently available.

As two men or two women in relationships we have no legal right to marry each other. Nor is there a box to check on our IRS 1040 giving us legal benefits for our love relationships. Two women walking down the street hand-in-hand cannot expect to receive the same benign indifference to the spectacle of their affection that a young straight couple can assume. A reporter in *Sports Illustrated Women* noted her surprise that there were gay male bullfighters in Mexico, demonstrating that as gay men we still cannot expect our masculinity to be judged by anything except the sexual conquest of women. There is still much that gay and lesbian people are waiting for.

Yet the promise that God is making all things new is fulfilled the moment we step out and proclaim the truth about ourselves. Our faith manifests the promise that God is resolved for the liberation of the whole creation when we make a commitment to each other before the whole community. We enjoy the fruits of the promise that there will be an end to hate and oppression when we sit arm-and-arm in movie theaters. We participate in the fulfillment of Christ's work when we measure ourselves as men and women, not by tired sex-roles, but by the integrity of our relationships and by the practice of our faith.

SILENCE

PRAYER

You have a will for me, Lord,
grant me knowledge of it,
and the strength to enact my faith.

Thursday of the First Week of Advent

PSALM

Open to me the gates of righteousness,
that I may enter through them
and give thanks to the Lord.
(Ps 118:19)

SCRIPTURE

Isaiah 26:1–6; Psalm 118:1, 8–9, 19–21, 25–27; Matthew 7:21, 24–27

MEDITATION

Today Isaiah shows us the gateway into the vision and promise of God. "Open the gates!" he says (Isa 26:2). In Matthew, Jesus tells us how to do it, "everyone then who hears these words of mine and acts on them will be like a wise man" (Mt 7:24). As we have seen all week, Isaiah describes the vision and promise while Jesus shows us how to manifest it.

Jesus also gives us a caution; not everyone who calls on the Lord's name will arrive at the Promised Land. I see many people who appear to call on the name of God and yet act, not out of the love of God, but rather out of hatred and homophobia. What effect does their hateful behavior have on me as I await the coming of Jesus? For me, the best way to make sense of the experience of others' hatred is to see it as a projection. What they hate is not me, but some fear in themselves that they project onto me. Often, when I react with anger towards them it is because I also have my own fear and lack of self-acceptance. When I respond in fear I internalize their fear and begin to behave in self-destructive ways. When I angrily condemn them I become the vain chanter of "Lord, Lord," myself while I do nothing to manifest the promise. The hard work of faith is to set aside my fear and respond to others out of the affirmation and love I owe myself.

As I await the fulfillment of my life I can act out of love and not fear. Then the gates open wide.

SILENCE

PRAYER

Lord, help me today to put aside my own anger and fear, and in the face of hate let me respond with the same love you promise me.

Friday of the First Week of Advent

PSALM

I believe that I shall see
the goodness of the Lord,
in the land of the living.
(Ps 27:13)

SCRIPTURE

Isaiah 29:17–24; Psalm 27:1, 4, 13–14; Matthew 9:27–31

MEDITATION

Isaiah and Matthew continue this week's theme of promise and fulfillment. Today, both include the metaphor of the blind seeing on that day when the divine is encountered. Blindness is a good metaphor for the physical and spiritual reality of our humanity. It is both an obstacle and the means by which we can obtain grace. When I see physically blind men and women negotiating their way in public I see an example of great faith.

Spiritual blindness is a far greater challenge to overcome than physical blindness. Physically blind men and women open all their senses to become aware of the world around them. When we are spiritually blind we shut our senses down to create a phony world where we can hide from the truth. Addiction, self-destructive behavior, manipulation of others, these are all signs of spiritual blindness. Recognizing our powerlessness over what we are afraid of and realizing that God's plan for us is to be happy, joyous, and free is the beginning of insight that leads to fulfillment of the promise.

For many gay men and lesbian women, coming out is the first step toward ending the spiritual blindness imposed by the closet.

Accepting our same-sex attraction as a gift and not a disorder is the next step. Finally, living our lives with dignity allows us to see and rejoice in the Holy One of Israel.

SILENCE

PRAYER

Holy One, cast your light into the dark areas of my life
that I may see and rejoice with you.

Saturday of the First Week of Advent

PSALM

Great is our Lord, and abundant in power;
God's understanding is beyond measure.
The Lord lifts up the downtrodden;
God casts wickedness to the ground.
(Ps 147:5–6)

SCRIPTURE

Isaiah 30:19–21, 23–36; Psalm 147:1–6; Matthew 9:35–10:1, 6–8

MEDITATION

Throughout this first week of Advent Isaiah has foretold the coming fulfillment of God's promise, and in the Gospels Jesus has shown us how to manifest this imminent reign. In today's readings the metaphor of the teacher helps us understand how God's promise is revealed. In Isaiah God is a hidden teacher who we will see and who will guide our steps. In Matthew Jesus sends out his disciples to teach us that God's realm is always at hand. We can ignore our teachers, however, and eat "the bread of adversity and the water of affliction" (Isa 30:20).

When I was a senior in high school my English teacher, Mr. Lewis, tried to teach me the truth about being gay. He took me to the theater and out to dinner and talked to me many times, always trying to demonstrate that there was more to being gay than dressing like Iggy Stardust and having anonymous sex in public restrooms. I did not want to learn. I did not want to accept the truth that was immediately available. So I spent another eighteen years trying to run from the fulfillment of God's promise in my life.

Mr. Lewis always shared his insights without any charge, as have many other gay men and lesbian women I have met throughout the years. Eventually, across time, I have been able to accept the gift of my sexuality. Now my days are seven times brighter than they were. My wounds are dressed. My scars have healed. My only regret is that Mr. Lewis died before this "dawn from on high" broke upon me. He never got to see the light come into my darkness.

SILENCE

PRAYER

Lord, help us to heed the teachers that you send us,
and to give thanks to them for carrying your message.

THE SECOND WEEK OF ADVENT: PREPARATION
The Second Sunday of Advent

PSALM

Read the Psalm twice, pausing for a few minutes between readings. Notice what word or phrase stands out for you.

Let me hear what God the Lord will speak,
for God will speak peace to the people,
to the faithful, to those who turn to God in their hearts.
(Ps 85:8)

SCRIPTURE

Read the appropriate texts depending on whether it is year A, B, or C. See "Reading Cycle for Advent and Christmas" (pp. 99–106). Notice what word or phrase holds your attention.

Catholic Lectionary	Revised Common Lectionary
Year A:	**Year A:**
Isa 11:1–10;	Isa 11:1–10;
Ps 72:1–2, 7–8, 12–13, 17;	Ps 72:1–7, 18–19;
Rom 15:4–9;	Rom 15:4–13;
Mt 3:1–12	Mt 3:1–12
Year B:	**Year B:**
Is 40:1–5, 9–11;	Isa 40:1–11;
Ps 85:9–14;	Ps 85: 1–2, 8–13;
2 Pt 3:8–14;	2 Pet 3:8–15a;
Mk 1:1–8	Mk 1:1–8
Year C:	**Year C:**
Bar 5:1–9;	Mal 3:1–4;
Ps 126:1–6;	Lu 1:68–79;
Phil 1:4–6, 8–11;	Phil 1:3–11;
Lk 3:1–6	Lk 3:1–6

MEDITATION

I have seen a man so dirty that his clothes, his hair, even his very person seemed to be constructed out of filth. I have seen other such men scouring public garbage cans looking for food. It's hard to imagine that a person dressed in rags, eating whatever refuse is at hand, is the one who will introduce me to someone whose shoe laces I am not fit to tie. And yet this is John the Baptist; a rag-wearing, bug-and-honey-eating, homeless engineer preparing the royal highway of the Lord. This second Sunday of Advent introduces us to the theme of preparation. Jesus is coming to fulfill his earthly ministry, and in Advent we wait and get ready for his arrival. Significantly, Jesus arrives first as a baby and then later as a common man introduced by a homeless person in the dessert. Jesus, and the fulfillment of God's vision, comes through the margins of society.

While I sleep out of doors only by choice and have never eaten garbage, as a gay person I do experience marginalization. While a homeless family can often find sympathy for their plight, gay men and lesbian women can experience being turned away from society, not because there is no room, but because we are often seen as nothing but hedonistic sex maniacs. Regardless of the lifestyle I choose to live, I can be greeted with "God Hates Fags," or I can have my love relationship reduced to nothing more than acts I perform in the privacy of my bedroom. From vitriolic conservatism to benign liberal indifference, I am reduced to a sex-motivated freak simply because I acknowledge the truth that I am gay.

Sometimes I think humans move too slowly to enact God's justice. The announcement has been made that same-sex love and attraction is neither a sin nor a sexual compulsion. Many have worked hard to prepare the way for gay men and lesbian women to live lives somewhere other than on the margins. Full acceptance has not yet come. God is waiting for everyone to catch up. It takes a long time to level mountains and fill in valleys. And it takes time for people to see the messenger in John and the truth of love in a same-sex relationship. I observe the process of leveling, filling, and preparing the road in my own life, and with patience I can also see that God's reign is at hand.

SILENCE

Sit in silence. Recall what words or phrases from the Scripture drew your attention as you were reading. Listen for what the readings and meditation are saying to you today. Answer these two questions: What are the texts and meditations saying to me today? What are the texts and meditation asking me to do or be today?

PRAYER

Lord, you come in unexpected ways
to show me that your gift is present now.
Help me to prepare myself for the path you have before me.

Monday of the Second Week of Advent

PSALM

Let me hear what God the Lord will speak,
for God will speak peace to the people,
to God's faithful, to those who turn to God in their hearts.
(Ps 85:8)

SCRIPTURE

Isaiah 35:1–10; Psalm 85:9–14; Luke 5:17–26

MEDITATION

The messianic fulfillment makes the desert bloom and restores the sick to health. Jesus shows us that faith is the door, or hole in the roof, which we go through to enter this messianic place.

One Sunday I was at a service sponsored by Dignity, a Catholic association for gay and lesbian persons. As part of the service healing prayers were offered. As the priest came down the aisle a man in front of me stood to receive healing. The priest asked each of us around him to place our hands on him while he prayed over the man. I do not know what need for healing this man communicated to the priest, but as the prayers were said the man began to cry. I could not tell if he was physically healed of any ailment, but I know from the catharsis of his experience, and of similar experiences in my own life, that faith gives us the strength to deal with difficult situations that previously baffled us.

While miraculous cures for AIDS, cancer, addiction, or any other form of human suffering are rare, there is a commonplace opportunity for healing always available. Healing comes when we turn to Jesus and ask for the gift of faith to persevere in the life God gives us. Living in the promise in our earthly life does not mean that we can get up and walk away from our problems. Rather it means that God is with us while we continue to deal with our problems and heal from our wounds.

SILENCE

PRAYER

Lord, grant me the faith

to accept the things I cannot change,
and the grace to see through my pain
to the reality of your promise of love.

Tuesday of the Second Week of Advent

PSALM

O sing to the Lord a new song;
sing to the Lord, all the earth.
sing to the Lord, bless God's name;
tell of the Lord's salvation from day to day.
(Ps 96:1–2)

SCRIPTURE

Isaiah 40:1–11; Psalm 96:1–3, 10–13; Matthew 18:12–14

MEDITATION

Today Isaiah announces the messenger of the Lord, "A voice cries out, 'In the wilderness prepare the way of the Lord'" (Isa 40:3). The period of our punishment is ending and now the desert will bloom. In Matthew, Jesus goes to look for a stray, because in the end none are to be lost.

"God Hates Fags." That is the meanest of the litanies of hate I often hear. "Hate the sin, but not the sinner" is the most devilish because it dehumanizes people into a collection of acts and then allows the speaker to indulge in an orgy of hate free from any obligation to God's commandment against judging others. Because I am gay, I often hear that most pernicious of litanies. Because I am human, I have the ability to apply it to those who express homophobia and hate that sin of theirs.

The word of God says that, "so it is not the will of your Father in heaven that one of these little ones should be lost" (Mt 18:14). God does not hate any part of the creation of love, and hatred is not a part of God's greatest commandment. The practice of Christian faith is to love other people. Hatred is not a Christian value, nor is it doing the will of God. Hating sin is the cheapest form of grace, because it means avoiding the hard work of loving someone we find difficult to care about. But it is in loving those "other" people that we prepare the way for the messianic promise.

SILENCE

PRAYER

Lord, help me with the difficult task of loving others, and not simply taking refuge in the easy grace of despising their homophobia.

Wednesday of the Second Week of Advent

PSALM

The Lord is merciful and gracious,
slow to anger,
and abounding in steadfast love.
(Ps 103:8)

SCRIPTURE

Isaiah 40:25–32; Psalm 103:1–4, 8, 10; Matthew 11:28–30

MEDITATION

Isaiah asks, who is like our God? Who has the strength, the power, the understanding of our God? Who has the constancy of support for us, as does our God? In Matthew Jesus gives us the "how" by providing us with a place of rest and the capacity to lift up our faith if we go to him.

The Bible shows us the history of God's love and constancy. My response to God does not have that perfect constancy, but as I look back over the story of my own faith, even though I do not see perfection, I do see progress. The old issues are not obstacles any more. I no longer wonder if there is a God. Now I try to figure out how to negotiate the difficult terrain of life while practicing principles externally that internally I have accepted. It is not the "why" of belief I struggle with now, but the "how" of dealing with others in the church. How do I witness against the bigoted, sexist, racist, homophobic, phallocentric structures within the institutional church without falling victim to the very same fundamentalism that undergirds those sins?

The hard work of avoiding fundamentalism lies in my setting aside the easy enjoyment of my righteous indignation. Instead of concentrating on other people's errors, I try to focus on the positive model of Christ's gentle and humble heart. When I attempt to control others my burden is heavy. When I allow God to work out the details of the church's direction and pay attention to living with integrity as being my role in God's plan, my burden lightens considerably. I grow as I focus on the constancy of God's love. Living with integrity is how I help make the dessert bloom.

SILENCE

PRAYER

Lord, as I continue to grow in your will,
grant me the grace of a gentle and humble heart.

Thursday of the Second Week of Advent

PSALM

All your works shall give thanks to you, O Lord,
and all your faithful shall bless you.
They shall speak of the glory of your kingdom,
and tell of your power.
(Ps 145:10–11)

SCRIPTURE

Isaiah 41:13–20; Psalm 145:1, 9–13; Matthew 11:11–15

MEDITATION

Jacob, the worm, and Israel, the maggot, will become God's threshing-sledge, the tool of God's saving work. Jesus states that John the Baptist's message is the culmination of this Old Testament project. John prepares the way for the new relationship with Jesus.

Worms and maggots? How do we go from them to threshing-sledges? And John, a raggedy, bug-eater in the dessert is the culmination? There are times when God is weird. But then, of course, the worm and the maggot are a part of God's creation and fulfill their place in the divine economy. It is their work to break down what is dead and rotting to create new and fertile soil. It may seem an insult to compare humans to maggots, but in the fullness of who we are we share with the maggot a call to be ourselves so truly that we break down the dead images of what it is to be human and witness to the truth and perfection of our lives. The maggot glorifies God by being exactly what it was created to be. So does John with his rags and bugs; and in our husbandry as threshers, so do we.

What is true for John and maggots is true for us as well. Same-sex love is as much a part of God's creation and intention for us individually as maggotry and bug eating are for those called to those ways. To be openly, unabashedly, and affirmatively gay or lesbian is God's plan for us. As a gay person, I thresh the way of the Lord by winnowing self-hate and cultivating myself as the wonderful, gay creation that I am.

SILENCE

PRAYER

Lord, give me the strength to be the voice of affirmation, crying out in the wasteland of fear and self-doubt.

Friday of the Second Week of Advent

PSALM

Happy are those
who do not follow the advice of the wicked,
or take the path that sinners tread,
or sit in the seat of scoffers;
but their delight is in the law of the Lord.
(Ps 1:1–2a)

SCRIPTURE

Isaiah 48:17–19; Psalm 1:1–4, 6; Matthew 11:16–19

MEDITATION

If the ancient Hebrews had only listened to God they would have been flooded with the benefits of God's teaching. It seems that no matter how God brings the message to us we can always find reasons to reject it: it is either the insanity of John's fervor, or the degradation of Jesus' associations.

As a gay person I am also the bearer of a message about love, a message that is frequently rejected. As a gay man the reaction I get when I try to foster love in the world is that I am either a sissy whom nobody wants to have commerce with, or I am a person who engages in hedonistic debauchery. There are moments when I can experience God's exasperation with human beings' rejection of one another. That experience helps me understand God's exasperation with me when I do not act out of love.

As a gay man I am on society's margins. In my own life, however, I am at the center and society's center is on my margin. Just as I am often condemned, how often have I condemned God's representative, because the message was coming from my margins? If the greatest commandment is to love, and because love is what God created same-sex attraction to express, then I am ignoring the call to love when I choose to meet the homophobe, the right-wing Christian, the conservative Catholic, with anything other than the opportunity to love.

The announcement has been made. Christ is coming. I prepare the way of the Lord in my life by trying to love those hard-to-like people I encounter.

SILENCE

PRAYER

God, give me the capacity to see beyond the labels
to the simple human being so embraced by your love.

Saturday of the Second Week of Advent

PSALM

> Give ear, O Shepherd of Israel,
> you who lead Joseph like a flock!
> You who are enthroned upon the cherubim, shine forth.
> (Ps 80:1)

SCRIPTURE

Sirach 48:1–4, 9–11; Psalm 80:2–3, 15–19; Matthew 17:10–13

MEDITATION

In today's Old Testament text Elijah the prophet is a seminal person, able to close up heaven and bring down God's wrath. In Matthew Jesus tells us that Elijah has already returned in John the Baptist. John completed Elijah's work by announcing a new world order, one grounded in justice and love. God's wrath has been averted. In love, God became human. The capacity of God's love is so enormous that it outweighs God's righteous anger and is transformed into humility on our behalf. God will do anything, including becoming human, to love me.

I came out of the closet when I realized that being gay was about love and not about sex acts. My first experience of love outside the closet was an overwhelming sense of gratitude and love for God. I was driving home from work one day when it occurred to me how often I asked for God's love but now how I desperately wanted to love God in return. I knew how to hug and kiss another person, but now I wanted to learn how to offer love to God. As much as I had rejected and been rejected by the church I rejoiced when a friend told me to go to the house of God. I have delighted in trying to discern God's will, walk in God's ways, and glory in God's love of me ever since.

I continue to try and live out the principle that love received is love that can be shared by loving others, my partner, my friends, and my community. Elijah and John announce to me the depth and power of God's love. Jesus loves *me.* Jesus' love for me is manifested as a desire to love in return.

Silence

Prayer

Let me love you, Lord,
through praise, adoration, my partner, and my community.

THE THIRD WEEK OF ADVENT: JOY
The Third Sunday of Advent, Gaudete Sunday

Psalm

Read the Psalm twice, pausing for a few minutes between readings.
Notice what word or phrase stands out for you.

Praise the Lord!
Praise the Lord, O my soul!
I will praise the Lord as long as I live;
I will sing praises to my God all my life long.
(Ps 146:1–2)

Scripture

Read the appropriate texts depending on whether it is year A, B, or C. See
"Reading Cycle for Advent and Christmas" (pp. 99–106). Notice what
word or phrase holds your attention.

Catholic Lectionary	Revised Common Lectionary
Year A:	**Year A:**
Isa 35:1–6, 10;	Isa 35:1–10;
Ps 146:6–10;	Ps 146:5–10;
Jas 5:7–10;	Jas 5:7–10;
Mt 11:2–11	Mt 11:2–11
Year B:	**Year B:**
Isa 61:1–2, 10–11;	Isa 61:1–4, 8-11;
Lk 1:46–50, 53–54;	Ps 126;
1 Thess 5:16–24;	1 Thess 5:16–24;
Jn 1:6–8, 19–28	Jn 1:6–8, 19–28

Year C:
Zeph 3:14-18;
Isa 12:2-6;
Phil 4:4-7;
Lk 3:10-18

Year C:
Zeph 3:14-20;
Isa 12:2-6;
Phil 4:4-7;
Lk 3:7-18

MEDITATION

The Third Sunday of Advent is known as "Gaudete Sunday" from the traditional opening antiphon for the service: *Gaudete in Domino Semper* (Rejoice in the Lord always). On this day we recognize that we are more than half way through the waiting period for Christ. The first two readings of the day reflect this call for joy, while the Gospel shows us John announcing that Jesus is already among us, unrecognized, and about to be made visible.

On Gaudete Sunday 2002 I was at a Mass presided over by a Franciscan father. He announced to us that this was such a wonderful day because priests everywhere get to come out and wear their pink chasubles. Everyone nodded. I almost fell out of my pew. But I saw the wonderful truth of what he was saying. As gay and lesbian people, we are not at full social and ecclesial acceptance yet. But when we come out openly, and joyfully proclaim who we are, then we are more than half way there. We are a part of God's creation and plan too. Our call is to express the joy of same-sex love.

Jesus is among us. As we accept who we are and reach out in joy and confidence as gay men and lesbian women, we will encounter the love of Christ.

SILENCE

Sit in silence. Recall what words or phrases from the Scripture drew your attention as you were reading. Listen for what the readings and meditation are saying to you today. Answer these two questions:

What are the texts and meditations saying to me today? What are the texts and meditation asking me to do or be today?

PRAYER

Thank you, O Lord,
for putting me in the pink today,
that I may gaily proclaim your coming.

Monday of the Third Week of Advent

PSALM

Make me to know your ways, O Lord;
teach me your paths.
Lead me in your truth and teach me,
for you are the God of my salvation.
(Ps 25:4–5a)

SCRIPTURE

Numbers 24:2–7, 15–17; Psalm 25:4–9; Matthew 21:23–27

MEDITATION

Baalam saw the Messiah coming, not in the present, but as "a star shall come out of Jacob" (Num 24:17). John the Baptist announced that the one long-awaited was immanently here in Jesus. The chief priests and elders challenged Jesus' authority because it threatened their own authority. The truth is often self-evident, but when human authority meets truth the status quo is threatened and often those in power will not step out of their entrenched privilege to grasp the truth.

Being gay is my self-evident truth. I have two straight friends who are self-described Ronald Reagan Republicans. They can embrace me as a gay man because they are certain of who they are and what they believe. They walk conservatively in orthodox truth and they recognize and embrace my truth. Other people in my life want me to be silent because they cannot handle the truth of who I am. They are afraid because they are not certain of who they are and what they believe and they want to hang on to what little they have. They have confused conservatism, which is one path to truth, with orthodoxy itself.

Orthodoxy is neither liberal nor conservative. Both positions have perspectives on the truth. Both can gain ascendancy and become the status quo. When this happens, conservatives and liberals alike can confuse their position with orthodoxy and declare their position as the only truth.

Jesus did not confirm the status quo when it refused the truth of God's message of justice and love, and neither will I. Whether it is a conservative expressing homophobia and distorting the Christian message with hate or a liberal refusing to acknowledge the basic humanity of a conservative opponent, I seek to be faithful to Jesus' example of what it is to be fully human. Jesus' way of truth is hard and narrow, and we have to carve the path for ourselves.

SILENCE

PRAYER

O Lord, teach me your truth.
Help me to see my path to you and be unafraid along the way.

Tuesday of the Third Week of Advent

PSALM

This poor soul cried, and was heard by the Lord,
and was saved from every trouble.
(Ps 34:6)

SCRIPTURE

Zephaniah 3:1–2, 9–13; Psalm 34:2–3, 6–7, 17–19, 23; Matthew 21:28-32

MEDITATION

The truth is seldom what we expect. As we see in Zephaniah, those who will find favor with God are the humble and the lowly. And in

Matthew we see that those who righteously proclaim that they will do what is right often do not, while those who are despised or on the margin are the ones who do what is right.

According to society my choosing to be openly gay is not doing what I am supposed to do. I should be like my straight brothers and choose marriage and children. Yet I am in a monogamous, committed relationship open to the creative and procreative possibilities God chooses to make manifest in our relationship.

Today I see popular culture using marriage between a man and a woman as nothing more than an excuse for a variety of silly television game shows. Even though the gender arrangements are correct, I think the straight brothers and sisters involved are not portraying the intended beauty of marriage.

Jesus often turns things on their head. I may not be a part of the group who always seems to be doing what they are supposed to do, but I can see the affirmation of truth in my love relationship, as queer as it is!

SILENCE

PRAYER

God, let me not be afraid to proclaim the truth of love,
even when it is not in conformity with everyone else around me.

Wednesday of the Third Week of Advent

PSALM

Lord, you were favorable to your land;
you restored the fortunes of Jacob.
You forgave the iniquity of your people;
you pardoned all their sin.
(Ps 85:1–3)

SCRIPTURE

Isaiah 45:6–8, 18, 21–25; Psalm 85:9–14; Luke 7:18–23

MEDITATION

Today Isaiah outlines the range of God's creative and dramatic power. In Luke we find that Jesus responds to the Baptist's questions with another outline of great deeds. God does not simply ask for our awe and obedience. God gives us proof of divine love and then asks us to use our own observation to find out who God is in relation to our lives.

From today's readings it appears that Christian faith could be based on empirical data. That would be wonderful, as it is fundamentally easier to follow directions than it is to discern the subtleties of God's will. But what Jesus is doing here is more oblique than that. He doesn't say, "I made the blind see." He says, "The blind see again." We have to make the connection between Jesus and the blind man through faith. Faith guides by asking questions. Even the Ten Commandments demand inquiry rather than slavish obedience. The best use of the Bible is as a series of ongoing questions that keep going deeper into life.

A few years ago when I felt I was falling to pieces I went to the biblical book of Job for answers. What I found there was several weeks' worth of reading and rereading, of arguing and struggling with God. My first reaction to the story of Job was that God was a bully and a sore loser. By the end of the process I found that God—through Job—was giving me a safe place to vent my anger and despair. Instead of attacking others or succumbing to self-loathing I could stand before God and cry out the great existential "Why?"

While I may have been unrealistic to demand definitive answers from God, I was not wrong to challenge what was happening to me. As with Job, God answered. And the answer was that God loved me. When the drama was done I realized that I still had everything I thought I had lost when I came out, and as time went by I saw an increase in my life. The fundamental error of making the Bible a rule list did not produce the joyful life I have today. Rather, my agreeing to be a part of the messy process of life and my assurance of God's love for me allows me to live the good news that the blind receive their sight, the lame walk, and the dead are raised up again.

SILENCE

PRAYER

When I cry out from the depths hear me, Lord,
that I may continually praise you for your steadfast love.

Thursday of the Third Week of Advent

PSALM

As for me, I said in my prosperity,
"I shall never be moved."
By your favor, O Lord,
 you had established me as a strong mountain;
you hid your face;
I was dismayed.
(Ps 30:6–7)

SCRIPTURE

Isaiah 54:1–10; Psalm 30:2, 4–6, 11–13: Luke 7:24–30

MEDITATION

Isaiah tells us that God's steadfast love will never depart from us, that
God will not abandon us and that God is always ready to gather us
back "with great compassion" (Isa 54:7). In Luke Jesus tells us how
John plays a role in God's steadfast love. Through the baptism offered
by John, God is still gathering. Even so, the Pharisees "rejected God's
purpose" (Lk 7:30) by refusing John and refusing baptism.

Why would the Pharisees and the lawyers reject baptism? I think
Isaiah has the answer. As Isaiah tells it, those who are restored to God
are the barren, the shamed, the disgraced, the widowed. The marginal
people of society are being reclaimed by God. Politicians and lawyers
are not marginal people and they are not willing to become marginalized.

I am gay, which in our society puts me in a marginal group. I am
also a university educated, white man. If I am willing to "pass," my
education, race, and gender put me somewhere at the top of the

social ladder. My life is a constant movement back and forth between centrality and marginalization. There are times when I see the clear benefits of being on the top of the social ladder. But I have also noticed that it is when I am open and vulnerable and not in command, that God enters my life most powerfully. It is scary to give up control and assume a role at the bottom, which is why I can understand the Pharisees and the lawyers not wanting to give up what they have. Being open and vulnerable and having faith is sometimes discomfiting, but ultimately fulfilling.

SILENCE

PRAYER

Gracious God, command is a responsibility you sometimes give me. Give me the privilege to be vulnerable at the bottom as well.

Friday of the Third Week of Advent

PSALM

May God be gracious to us and bless us
and may God's face shine upon us,
that your way may be known upon earth,
your saving power among all nations.
(Ps 67:1–2)

SCRIPTURE

Isaiah 56:1–3, 6–8; Psalm 67:2–3, 5, 7–8; John 5:33–36

MEDITATION

The Baptist is the witness to Jesus' mission, but Jesus' work is clearly a greater sign of God's will. And in Isaiah we see that this mission is available for all, as God says, "my house shall be called a house of prayer for all peoples" (Isa 56:7b).

For ten years I lived in a predominantly Black neighborhood and attended the local parish church where I was the minority. I found that African-American Catholic worship expressed a physical exuberance that was different from the mental intensity of the white congregations in which I grew up. I believed it *viscerally* when the cantor sang, "I rejoiced when they said, 'let us go up to the house of the Lord'" because everyone around me was visibly rejoicing!

I knew what it meant to be a gay man in America because being around straight people constantly highlighted my status. But it was not until I spent several years living and worshiping in a Black community, and seeing the contrast in worship styles that I began to understand what it means to be a white man in America. I began to see that despite the oppression I experienced as a gay man, I was still the beneficiary of the structures of racism that maintain white male power. And I saw how I benefited from the structural sin of racism.

I cannot completely escape corporate sin in my life. I will always be the beneficiary of a system that privileges white people like me, but I try to acknowledge this condition of structural sin and recognize that being the beneficiary of white male privilege does not save me. Rather, I have to step away from these privileges and be humble before them in order to make myself open to the saving grace of God. I am grateful that God's work is about gathering all people and I am grateful that God's church is intended as a house of prayer for all, including me.

SILENCE

PRAYER

God, thank you for the gifts Black people give.
And thank you for the wisdom of the African-American experience.

FOURTH WEEK OF ADVENT: INCARNATION
December 17

PSALM

O come, Thou Wisdom from on High.
You govern all creation with your strong and tender care.
Come and show your people the way to salvation.
(From the "O" antiphon for December 17)

SCRIPTURE

Genesis 49:2, 8–10; Psalm 72:3–4, 7–8, 17; Matthew 1:1–17

MEDITATION

In today's reading Genesis looks forward in time to announce the constant communion of humanity and God. Matthew looks backward in time from the birth of Christ to show how this constancy was made manifest through the tree of Jesse. Christians are an historically-minded people and God uses that historical mindset to further demonstrate divine love.

Many people ask me why I am a Christian or why I stay in the Catholic Church considering all the institutional homophobia found there. My response is that I am not a one-issue person. There is a universality and a historicity that connects me to God and humanity and that keeps me in the church. I am a part of the constancy that today's readings point to. As I look back across my life, church history, and scripture, I see the faithful witness of gay people. Father Mychal Judge, the fire department chaplain who died in the September 11 terrorist act, proved that a gay man could show strength and courage in the face of violence. My friends Jack and Peter showed me how gay men can live in a relationship as good Catholics. Michael Lewis, my high school teacher, was an example for me of how being gay takes courage and is not for sissies. St. Anselm, who in the eleventh century affirmed the naturalness of gay love, was made a doctor of the church. And finally in First Samuel we find Jonathan and David, whose biblical witness to same-sex love resounds through time.

God comes to earth through history and in Jesus. Jesus' message of God's constant love is expressed by the whole church throughout history. This message of love is for all. Even me.

SILENCE

PRAYER

God, help me to remember those gay and lesbian Christians who have gone before and to give thanks for their witness to your love.

December 18

PSALM

O come, O come, great Lord of might.
Come stretch out your mighty hand and set us free.
(From the "O" antiphon for December 18)

SCRIPTURE

Jeremiah 23:5–8; Psalm 72:1, 12–13, 18–19; Matthew 1:18–24

MEDITATION

Today Jeremiah is prophesying to the Hebrews who have been scattered from their home and are living in the fear and pain of exile. The gospel shows us Joseph as he is faced with the apparent disgrace of Mary's pregnancy. The readings begin with isolation, pain, and scandal.

I am writing these meditations in the midst of what has come to be known as the Catholic clergy sexual-abuse scandal. It has not been a happy time for the Catholic Church in America, with scores of people testifying to the abuse they suffered, and the sight of priests and bishops humiliated for their roles in creating or covering up these crimes. The scandal has produced an effort in some quarters to scapegoat gay men in order to distract attention from the bishops' malfeasance. This has intensified the feeling of exile felt by many gay Catholic priests, religious, and laity. But I cannot help but feel hope from Jeremiah today. "The days are surely coming, says the Lord, when I will raise up for David a righteous branch" (Jer 23:5). The truth that is emerging from this scandal is that everyone is finally recognizing how many gay men there are in the priesthood and religious life, a number that far outweighs the number of abusive priests, and people are recognizing just how much good these men have contributed to the church. Efforts to deny gay men access to the priesthood are already seen as misguided and are serving to highlight the need to reform the priesthood and the church hierarchy's misunderstanding of human sexuality.

There have been other scandals in the church. Mary was an unmarried woman, pregnant by someone other than her betrothed. Joseph, that betrothed, was a descendant of Solomon who was born of the scandalous adultery between King David and Uriah's wife, Bathsheba. Jesus' earthly life culminated in the scandal of the cross. God seems to use human scandal as the birthplace for divine salvation. So while I wait out this scandal, saddened by the pain of its victims, I see only hope for the future of the church.

SILENCE

PRAYER

Surprising God, grace me with the virtue of Hope,
that I may learn from the Holy Spirit
when I hear her voice.

December 19

PSALM

O come, O Flower of Jesse's stem,
a sign for all people,
let nothing keep you from coming to our aid.
(From the "O" antiphon for December 19)

SCRIPTURE

Judges 13:2–7, 24–25a; Psalm 71:3–6, 16–17; Luke 1:5–25

MEDITATION

Today in Judges and Luke we see the foreshadowing of Jesus' birth in the birth of a hero, Samson, who is to save the Israelites and in the birth of a prophet, John, who is to announce the way of the Lord. A common element to both stories is the previous barrenness of John's and Samson's mothers. At that time barrenness would have been seen as a condemnation from God. Yet we see God once again transacting the economy of salvation through the disenfranchised, the marginal, the barren.

"If everyone were gay how could society continue?" I find it incredible that such a question is asked, but it is one that has been directed at me countless times. It is not a faith-informed question. A number of times in scripture we find people who appear to be incapable of procreating, not only having children, but participating with God in ways that guarantee the continuity of our faith. In today's readings we have Samson's and John's parents and elsewhere in the Bible we have the story of Abraham and Sarah. God regularly works through supposedly impossible situations and unacceptable people.

Posterity is a part of being gay or lesbian. Not only do many gay men and lesbian women have children, but gay and lesbian male and female children are themselves the regular offspring of each generation's children. There is also a spiritual continuity of the gay and lesbian experience. We continue to reverence the life and work of such people as St. Anselm, Saints Perpetua and Felicity, and Michelangelo. God regularly uses the social outcast, the misfit, the barren woman to manifest the divine promise. As lesbian and gay people we also are vehicles of God's activity and we have shown that, like Samson and John, we can work for and announce God's holy presence.

SILENCE

PRAYER

O Lord, let my voice resound with your promise
as I do the part you give to me to complete your plan.

December 20

PSALM

O Come, O Key of David, O royal power of Israel,
break down the walls of death for those in darkness
and lead your captive people free.
(From the "O" antiphon for December 20)

SCRIPTURE

Isaiah 7:10–14; Psalm 24:1–6; Luke 1:26–38

MEDITATION

In today's readings the foreshadowing of the Christmas miracle continues. Isaiah fortells the birth of a son, Immanuel, and Luke observes the miracle happening. We also have Mary's great fiat, "let it be with me according to your word" (Lk 1:38).

One day while I was still in the process of coming out to myself and others, I was walking down a hill below my workplace when I was overcome with a wonderful sense of freedom. By accepting the reality that I am gay as being God's will for me I became free of the fear and self-loathing that I had previously felt. I stopped walking and just stared for a time, incredulous at how liberated I finally felt. I realized how Mary's act of faith makes her the preeminent model of Christian conduct. The courage of countless men and women who openly affirm that they are gay is my model for making Mary's fiat a part of my life. Not by my choice, but by God's word, am I gay.

Jesus Christ came to set us free from the bondage of sin. I came out around Christmas and was filled with gratitude and a desire to love God. By accepting God's word for me I was finally able to experience the incarnation of same-sex love.

SILENCE

PRAYER

Loving God, let it be done to me according to your word,
that I may delight in your will and walk in your ways,
to the glory of your holy name.

December 21

PSALM

O come, Dayspring, splendor of eternal light,
come shine on those who dwell in darkness
and guide our feet into the way of peace.
(From the "O" antiphon for December 21)

SCRIPTURE

Song of Songs 2:8–14 OR Zephaniah 3:14–18; Psalm 33:2–3,
11–12, 20–21; Luke 1:39–45

MEDITATION

Our readings today highlight the joy we feel as the incarnation of
God's love grows near. As the Song of Songs recounts, our joy is like
the anticipation we feel at a lover's approach, or the joy a group of
people feels when delivered from a grave threat. Even the unborn
John feels joy when in the presence of his cousin Jesus.

Several nights a week my partner works late. That gives me time
to myself, time for reading or writing or meeting with a spiritual
group to which I belong. Then there is the wait for him to come
home. I may prepare for his arrival by cleaning the kitchen or doing
laundry or any of a number of activities that make our house homey.
Joy begins to emerge as I anticipate his imminent arrival. My heart
leaps, just like a young gazelle, "bounding over the hills," when I
hear his car pull into the driveway or his horn beep as he lets me
know that he is home.

When I am loved I taste love as I wait for the physical embodi-
ment of my lover. Absence highlights the love, and anticipation of his
arrival produces joy. This is how I feel now, just days away from the
celebration of the arrival of Jesus Christ and God's love in my life.

SILENCE

PRAYER

In joy let me receive you, O Lord,
so that in you my happiness will be complete.

December 22

PSALM

O come, Desire of all the nations, the joy of every heart, come and save us who you have fashioned from the dust. (From the "O" antiphon for December 22)

SCRIPTURE

1 Samuel 1:24–28; 1 Samuel 2:1, 4–8; Luke 1:46–56

MEDITATION

In today's readings both Hannah and Mary give thanks to God for their children. Both children are consecrated to God and both women are remembered for their faith and willingness to fulfill the will of God in their lives.

I recognize that there is more to a woman's contribution to society than bearing and raising children. I sense this because of my life as a childless gay man and because of the witness of my many childless, lesbian sisters. There is more to our lives than begetting children. The same is true for Mary as well. Mary has not been called blessed through all these generations simply because she was the vehicle for the birth of a baby. Mary's proclamation in today's Gospel says that she recognizes the greatness of God, "for he has looked with favor on the lowliness of his servant" (Lk 1:48). It is because of Mary's willingness to be the instrument of God's will that she is venerated. Presumably, God could have used Mary's baby-making capacity without her consent. But it is her fiat—"let it be with me as according to your word" (Lk 1:38)—that allows her spirit to rejoice. This is not deny the value of motherhood and fatherhood, but it is to exalt the willingness of the individual to choose to do what is right, according to God's will for that person.

The decision to make a child, or to openly declare same-sex love, or to accept consecrated life with chastity is all blessed because each of these decisions demonstrates the integrity of the individual. There is no integrity in a callous disregard for procreation, sex, or vows. But there is integrity in the willingness to accept and affirm God's will that we generate and manifest love and joy in our lives.

SILENCE

PRAYER

Holy is your name, O Lord, let me call upon your faithful love that extends from age to age.

December 23

PSALM

O come, O come, Emmanuel,
desire of the nations,
Savior of all people,
come and set us free.
(from the "O" antiphon for December 23)

SCRIPTURE

Malachi 3:1–4, 23–24; Psalm 25:4–5, 8-10, 14; Luke 1:57–66

MEDITATION

When God is with us—Emmanuel—miracles happen. Parents and children are reconciled; communities are saved. Even the mute will speak. Today's readings show us that as we approach the incarnate God—Jesus—wondrous things begin to happen.

I spent years trying to be straight and trying to be an atheist. Difficult circumstances produced enough pain in my life to lead me back to the church, and I spent several more years exploring various faith traditions. When I made an adult commitment to Catholic faith I finally found the courage to come out and be openly gay. To be honest was to recognize the reality of my feelings. To have integrity was to be open about who I am. To experience love was to take the risk of loving in the special way God created for me. On my path, as I approached Christ, I accepted the miracle of being gay.

There are many faith traditions and spiritual paths. As I honestly follow my path towards the mystery of God the promises begin to come true.

SILENCE

PRAYER

Gracious God, you have been the light along the way.
Help me to thoroughly follow the path you have laid for me.

December 24

PSALM

By the tender mercy of our God,
the dawn from on high will break upon us,
to give light to those who sit in darkness and in the shadow of death,
to guide our feet into the way of peace.
(Lk 1:78–79, "Benedictus")

SCRIPTURE

2 Samuel 7:1–5, 8–12, 14, 16; Psalm 89: 2–7, 27, 29; Luke 1:67–79

MEDITATION

Zechariah was struck dumb when he doubted God. When his son
John was born Zechariah spoke again and his first words were praise
for what God is about to do for us in the incarnation. Zechariah's
canticle, known also as the "Benedictus" from its first word in Latin,
is a part of the church's Morning Prayer in the Liturgy of the Hours.
It is a beautiful proclamation of the Christian promise.

Zechariah was a priest and had a responsibility for orderly worship
in his community. He was also a married man. In every way he was
a part of the mainstream. His son John, however, was not. John was
special. His role was to enter the dessert, an area on the margins of
civilization, and there, dressed in animal skins and eating weird food,
prepare the way of the Lord. John's life, in contrast to his father's,
was decidedly queer. God regularly uses queer people to enact the
divine promise.

My father and mother easily fit into the mainstream. When I tried
living in the mainstream—with all its accoutrements of house, wife,

career, car, etc.—I found myself alienated from God. The more I move away from the center to the margins the closer I get to God. It is in the marginal, the outsider, the queer that we find the truth. This does not mean that gay and lesbian people are closer to God than straight people are. I have a center in my life where I can allow materialism, social conformity, and status to block my access to God. It is in the margins of my personal life where I encounter God; just as my straight father does. The incarnate mystery involves my radical acceptance of the queer as the place where the divine is encountered. I will not find God in my materially successful center, but in the vulnerable edges of my life where the reality of God is made flesh.

SILENCE

PRAYER

God, keep me at the edges, away from the seduction of the center that I may love queerly like the Baptist.

The Fourth Sunday of Advent

(To be used on the Sunday following the week containing December 17)

PSALM

Read the Psalm twice, pausing for a few minutes between readings. Notice what word or phrase stands out for you.

O come, Desire of Nations,
joy of every human heart,
come and save us and transform our lives.
(From the "O" antiphon for December 22)

SCRIPTURE

Read the appropriate texts depending on whether it is year A, B, or C. See "Reading Cycle for Advent and Christmas" (pp. 99–106). Notice what word or phrase holds your attention.

Catholic Lectionary	Revised Common Lectionary
Year A:	Year A:
Isa 7:10–14;	Isa 7:10–16;
Ps 24:1–6;	Ps 80:1–7, 17–19;
Rom 1:1–7;	Rom 1:1–7;
Mt 1:18–24	Mt 1:18–25
Year B:	Year B:
2 Sam 7:1–5, 8b–12, 16;	2 Sam 7:1–11, 16;
Ps 89:2–5, 27, 29;	Ps 126;
Rom 16:25–27;	Rom 16:25–27;
Lk 1:26–38	Lk 1:26–38
Year C:	Year C:
Mic 5:1–4;	Mic 5:2–5a;
Ps 80:2–3, 15–16, 18–19;	Ps 80:1–7;
Heb 10:5–10;	Heb 10:5–10;
Lk 1:39–45	Lk 1:39–45

MEDITATION

The Angel Gabriel announces the coming incarnation of Christ to
Mary. This fulfills the promise made to David that his dynasty will
rule forever. The readings today also explore the question of where
and how to worship God. David, secure now in his new palace, wants
to build God a permanent home. But God tells him that his presence
will be with David and his line and God does not need a cedar-wood
resting place. Ultimately, despite Solomon's construction of the
Temple, we see that the true house of God is in the incarnation. The
physical location of the presence of God is in our own being.

A gay Christian friend of mine once told me about a question he
was asked, "Is it a sin to go to the baths?" In reply he asked the ques-
tioner if he would be comfortable taking Jesus into the baths with
him. The answers to questions like these demand individual discern-

ment. I sometimes want a respite from the presence of God, generally because of an issue about which I experience shame. Cheap morality answers the question of shame with simple avoidance. However, the hard work of building a relationship with God does not produce a faith that avoids living, but one in which questions of sin and shame are approached, lived, and resolved by a dynamic interaction with the divine.

Jesus went to many places we might deem inappropriate and consorted with many people thought to be perverse. Jesus himself was even accused of being a drunkard. Jesus was not afraid to go into places or be with people that society condemned with shame. Avoiding real life was never Jesus' answer, and neither should it be ours. Embracing Jesus wherever I am is how I build a temple for God's praise with my body.

Silence

Sit in silence. Recall what words or phrases from the Scripture drew your attention as you were reading. Listen for what the readings and meditation are saying to you today. Answer these two questions: What are the texts and meditations saying to me today? What are the texts and meditation asking me to do or be today?

Prayer

Be with me in my doubts, fears and discomforts, God, that they may be the building blocks of my temple to your Glory.

Christmas December 25th, Solemnity of the Nativity of the Lord

The custom of major festivals lasting for several days is ancient and widespread in various cultures. The traditional Christmas season runs from the feast of Christ's birth on December 25 to the Feast of the Baptism of Our Lord, on the first Sunday after Epiphany (January 6, also known as Twelfth Night). The church regularly celebrates eight days as a continuation of the holy day during both the Christmas and Easter cycles and thus the days are frequently referred to as being within the Octave of Christmas.

PSALM

Glory to God in the highest heaven,
and on earth peace among those whom God favors!
(Luke 2:14)

SCRIPTURE

Catholic Lectionary	Revised Common Lectionary
Readings for the Vigil:	**Proper I:**
Isa 62:1–5;	Isa 9:2–7;
Ps 89:4–5, 16–17, 27, 29;	Ps 96;
Acts 13:16–17, 22–25;	Titus 2:11–14;
Mt 1:1–25	Lk 2:1–14
Readings for Midnight:	**Proper II:**
Isa 9:1–6;	Isa 62:6–12;
Ps 96:1–3, 11–13;	Ps 97;
Titus 2:11–14;	Titus 3:4–7;
Lk 2:1–14	Lk 2:8–20
Readings for Dawn:	**Proper III:**
Isa 62: 11–12;	Isa 52:7–10;
Ps 97:1, 6, 11–12;	Ps 98;
Titus 3:4–7;	Heb 1:1–4;
Lk 2:15–20	Jn 1:1–14
Readings for the Day:	
Isa 52:7–10;	
Ps 98:1–6;	
Heb 1:1–6;	
Jn 1:1–18	

MEDITATION

"The people who walked in darkness have seen a great light," says Isaiah (9:2a). And that light, the Word of God, who has been with us since the beginning, is now here among us. It is Jesus Christ, the "Wonderful Counselor, Mighty God, Everlasting Father, Prince of Peace" (Isa 9:6b).

The time for waiting is over. With both joy and anticipation we have prepared for Christ and Jesus has now come. It is time to celebrate the goodness of God. Both Christmas and Easter celebrate the redemptive work of Jesus Christ, although Christmas focuses on the Incarnation of God's love and its physical presence among us. Jesus has arrived to demonstrate that there is a perfection to humanity that is expressed through the varieties of love that God has created: family love, friendship love, parental love, children love, straight love, same-sex love, all the myriad ways in which humanity reflects God's love.

During this time we celebrate the eternal and central truth of Christian faith: God is love. Love in all of its manifestations is present in the world. As gay and lesbian people we can shout with joy that God has manifested divine love through us as well.

SILENCE

PRAYER

A child is born to me, a son given to me;
dominion is laid on Jesus' shoulder,
and Christ shall be called wonderful-counselor. For this I give thanks.
(Based on entrance antiphon for Mass During the Day, from Isaiah 9:6)

December 26, Memorial of Stephen, First Martyr

PSALM

You have taken heed of my adversities,
and have not delivered me into the hand of the enemy;
you have set my feet in a broad place.
(Ps 31:7b–8)

SCRIPTURE

Acts 6:8–10; Psalm 31:3–8, 17, 21; Acts 7:54–59; Matthew 10:17–22

MEDITATION

It seems odd that we prepare for the joy of the Christmas season and when it arrives we find ourselves contemplating the martyrdom of St. Stephen and hear Jesus' warning that we will be persecuted for his sake.

I remember a sense of liberation when I came out of the closet. It was like a weight lifted from my chest, allowing me to breathe deeply at last. But the joy of this manifestation of love was tempered by the realities of the world. I had to deal with my friends' and my family's re-evaluation of me as a gay man and I had to confront the opposition that I received from some. By accepting the gift of my creation, however, I found the words to speak about who I am and over time the truth strengthened me.

I encountered two different Sauls when I came out: a friend and a family member both persecuted me. It was sad to see them hold my enemy's coat when I was attacked. But I still have hope for their ultimate conversion as they stumble, blinded by their homophobia, on their own road to Damascus.

SILENCE

PRAYER

Jesus, as I celebrate the joy of your incarnation,
help me to forgive those who cause suffering by their spiritual blindness.

December 27, Feast of St. John, Apostle, Evangelist

PSALM

Blessed be the Lord,
for God has wondrously shown
steadfast love to me.
(Ps 31:21)

SCRIPTURE

1 John 1:1–4; Psalm 97:1–2, 5-6, 11–12; John 20:2–8

MEDITATION

How appropriate that the feast celebrating St. John, the disciple whom Jesus loved, should be held so close to the nativity of Jesus. In today's readings from 1 John and John, we have John's affirmation of the faith he had in Jesus. In the Gospel, John comes to believe fully when he sees the empty tomb, and in his first letter he demonstrates the ever-present nature of what he believes in: the love of God through Christ.

Love is a sacrament, a way that God comes to us. The capacity to love and be loved is given to us by God as a grace. This love from God has a spiritual and a material form and when we participate in it we are made complete. In his letter John writes so that "our joy may be complete" (1 Jn 1:4). John was a witness to the three days of Christ's passion, crucifixion, and death. As Jesus' beloved he was deprived of his lover. John is thought to be the first male disciple to reach Jesus' tomb, and when he saw it empty, he believed. By accepting Jesus' love in life, and by believing in his resurrection at the empty tomb, John is completed by Christ's love. So too are we, and when we acknowledge who we are and offer love to our beloved we are a witness to our completion. By loving my partner I fulfill the sacramental nature of love.

Giving and receiving love is a gift from God and it is worship of God. When I love my partner I experience God's fulfillment and I give praise for the gift of the wonderful man God has put into my life.

SILENCE

PRAYER

God, grant that I experience your love through love of others, facing all our tomorrows together for as long as you shall grant.

December 28, Feast of the Holy Innocents, Martyrs

PSALM

> If it had not been the Lord who was on our side,
> when our enemies attacked us,
> then they would have swallowed us up alive,
> when their anger was kindled against us;
> then the flood would have swept us away,
> the torrent would have gone over us;
> then over us would have gone
> the raging waters.
> (Ps 124:2–5)

SCRIPTURE

1 John 1:5—2:2; Psalm 124:2–8; Matthew 2:13–18

MEDITATION

Today we remember those who innocently suffered because of the hatred and fear of others. Herod's violent act demonstrates the results of the darkness John talks about in his letter. Without the light of God our depravity kills.

John says that we are to live in the light of God's truth. When we say that we are without sin, we deceive ourselves and the truth is not in us. When we pretend that we are not who we are, we deceive ourselves as well. The closet is a dark place of deception and fear. When we confess who we are we come into the light. But as we see with the Holy Innocents, simply being who we are, being active Christians who are honest about how God is incarnate within us, can result in our death. Coming out of the closet can lead to martyrdom.

Being honest can be costly to us and to others. Today I remember the voice of Mrs. Shepherd weeping for her child Matthew refusing to be comforted because he is no more.

SILENCE

Prayer

God, I pray for all those murdered for the truth of their sexuality. Bring them into the light of your salvation with affirmation of their great love.

December 29, Fifth Day Within the Octave of Christmas

Psalm

O sing to the Lord a new song;
sing to the Lord, all the earth.
Sing to the Lord, bless God's name!
(Ps 96:12a)

Scripture

1 John 2:3–11; Psalm 96:1–6; Luke 2:22–35

Meditation

Christ's incarnation is a manifestation of the promise of God's love as outlined in the first reading from John's letter. That promise has been with us since the beginning as attested to by Simeon who waited for a long time for the fulfillment of the promise in Jesus. The promise of God's love has arrived, and like Simeon, we can now go in peace. As John points out in his letter there are many still living in blindness. It is our task as faithful Christians to manifest the light of God's love.

One similarity I found between coming out of the closet and accepting Christian faith was an uncertainty about how to behave afterwards. What does it mean for me to be openly gay? What does it mean to be openly Christian? How does it affect my sense of self, my masculinity, and my interactions with others? Am I offensively flaunting myself when I proclaim Christian faith, and am I acting superior to others? Am I creating an inappropriate disturbance when I joke with my friends and act like a queen? Over time I have found that the answer to these questions lies in gratefulness and humility. I am grateful for the gift of faith that God has given me and I am humbled by the magnificence of love that I find with my partner.

As I grow more grateful and humble, if light is shining from me, it is God's light. I am the instrument and not the source.

SILENCE

PRAYER

Gracious God, make me the instrument of your love.
And where there is darkness and hate, let your light and love shine through me.

December 30, Sixth Day Within the Octave of Christmas

PSALM

Let the heavens be glad, and let the earth rejoice;
let the sea roar, and all that fills it;
let the field exult, and everything in it.
Then shall all the trees of the forest sing for joy before the Lord;
for God is coming.
(Ps 96:11–13a)

SCRIPTURE

1 John 2:12–17; Psalm 96:7–10; Luke 2:36–40

MEDITATION

John's letter poses a conundrum. "Do not love the world," he says, "or the things in the world . . . for all that is in the world—the desire of the flesh, the desire of the eyes, the pride in riches—comes not from the Father but from the world" (1 Jn 2:15a, 16). John seems to suggest that love is supposed to be some spiritual act that flies above the mundane and messy realities of life, as if somehow we are supposed to ignore what is around us and not let it trouble or distract us. What distresses me is that I do not know how to separate myself from the cares of the world and live in a pure realm of love and spirit. The material world and the people in it always confound me.

I found the answer to this puzzle about how to live in the world in Luke. Anna, like Simeon in yesterday's reading, had been waiting for the consolation of Israel. The love and hope she and Simeon expressed was general and theoretical until the birth of Jesus. Once their hope was made incarnate they could love the world in a concrete way. Anna could now talk directly to "all who were looking for the redemption of Jerusalem" (Lk 2:38b). Jesus *is* the healthy expression of concrete love in the world.

"I love you, but I'm not in love with you." That is a classic break-up line formulated so that the speaker can try to maintain the privileges of love while being extricated from the messy responsibilities of love. This expression is similar to the expression "hate the sin, but love the sinner," wherein the person can indulge in an orgy of hatred while still maintaining a posture of Christian love. I have been on the giving and receiving end of both statements and know they are not expressions of concrete love because they are about distancing me from another person. I have not found a way of expressing a concrete love that is somehow ethereal and disengaged from the material world of family members, partners, friends, neighbors, and communities. I find that when I try to express love spiritually without the messy and very concrete entanglement of organized religion I wind up talking about generic responses to ideal circumstances that never happen. But when I have to deal with my own dysfunctional reality and that of other people in the pew or neighborhood, then I am forced to do the hard work of real loving.

When an old woman in my parish made a hash of Morning Prayer every day I had to come to terms with what community worship and love of neighbor meant for me. I even had to stay away from church for a while as an appropriate response to my anger. When I dealt with a Jesuit father who claimed he could accept gay men as long as we did not question the hierarchy's truncated explanation of who we are, I was forced to exercise charity, patience, and forgiveness. When I am attacked by homophobes who act like expressing hatred *is* being Christian I have to remember that defending myself does not mean tearing them down. Concrete love takes work and concrete love is messy. Loving my partner is concrete love and a false call to chastity is a faithless response to same-sex attraction.

SILENCE

PRAYER

> Help me in my daily love,
> that I may be embroiled in the concrete love of others
> and not removed by the theoretical love of all.

December 31, Seventh Day Within the Octave of Christmas

PSALM

> Say among the nations, "The Lord is king!
> The world is firmly established;
> it shall never be moved."
> (Ps 96:10)

SCRIPTURE

1 John 2:18–21; Psalm 96:1–2, 11–13; John 1:1–18

MEDITATION

Today in the readings we have both Christ and the Antichrist. In the Gospel we see that from the beginning Christ was with, in, and through God, and in John's letter we see that we are in the "final hour" when the Antichrist is coming. The truth has been with us from the first, and the assault on truth has begun. The standard understanding of the Antichrist is of an End Time figure that presages the culmination of Christ's work on earth. At the same time the reign of God is always at hand and the denial of Jesus' truth is the anti-Christian position. Through Christ we are always at the beginning and the end of the historical salvation project.

John says that accepting the truth saves us and that denying it is how we succumb to the Antichrist. Acceptance and denial, liberation and suppression, self-acceptance and self-loathing, these are all part of what John is telling us. The challenge I faced was not just to be honest about being gay, but to find a way to witness to a gay Christian truth. The easy part was reading books, asking questions, and memorizing statements that affirmed that neither the Bible nor the historical (as opposed to recent) traditions of Christian faith denigrated same-sex love. The hard part was, and still is, overcoming the fear of public witness.

I still falter and sometimes when the moment of truth comes I still run back toward the closet. But I pray for the courage to admonish the woman who says "gays recruit," and to proclaim loudly "liar" when the man tells me that homosexuality is an abomination.

SILENCE

PRAYER

Give me strength to witness to the truth,
that I may proclaim the saving love of Jesus Christ.

January 1, Solemnity of the Blessed Virgin Mary, Mother of God

PSALM

The earth has yielded its increase;
God, our God, has blessed us.
May God continue to bless us;
let all the ends of the earth revere God.
(Ps 67:6–7)

SCRIPTURE

Numbers 6:22–27; Psalm 67:2–8; Galatians 4:4–7; Luke 2:16-21

MEDITATION

Today's commemoration of Mary asks two questions. First, why do we call Mary the "Mother of God," and second, of what importance is this designation? During a visit prior to the birth of Jesus, Mary's cousin Elizabeth called Mary "mother of my Lord," so there is scriptural reference to this title. As a matter of Christian faith, the title of "Theotokos" or "Mother of God" was defined at the Council of Ephesus in 431. This title was based on a tradition that dates back to

St. Hippolytus in the third century who asked those seeking to join the church: "Do you believe in Christ Jesus, the Son of God, who was born by the Holy Spirit of the Virgin Mary?" The ancient tradition of both the Eastern and Western branches of the church is that God chooses powerless and weak people to demonstrate God's faithfulness. Mary, a young unwed girl, stands out as one who confidently hoped for and received salvation from God. God affirms the marginalized by establishing the new plan of salvation through them, and Mary is the primary model for this project.

So how does this model work for me as a gay man? Mary's fruitfulness has traditionally been understood as being made manifest by an act of faith and not a sexual act. Mary models how we can all be progenitors through acts of acceptance and faith. While these acts do not produce children, they do produce love.

I could have a biological child, many lesbian women and gay men do, but I know that I also give birth to a future when I model Christian integrity for younger people. I can affirm life by demonstrating for the gay teen working at the local IHOP that two gay men can have a fulfilling relationship. And just as I learned about relationships from older gay couples who learned from gay people before them, I can be a part of the great chain of life that goes back to before Jonathan and David and goes forward through all time by the creating will of God.

SILENCE

PRAYER

Let it be done to me according to your Word,
that I may be an instrument of your love.

January 2

PSALM

O sing to the Lord a new song,
for God has done marvelous things.
All the ends of the earth have seen

the victory of our God.
(Ps 98: 1a, 3b)

SCRIPTURE

1 John 2:22–28; Psalm 98:1–4; John 1:19–28

MEDITATION

In today's readings John suggests that the essential element of Christian faith is really quite simple: "Let what you heard from the beginning abide in you. If what you heard from the beginning abides in you, then you will abide in the Son and in the Father" (1 Jn 1:24). Often our human difficulty lies in not seeing God in front of us—a situation John points out in the gospel when the Baptist indicates that the Promised One is among the people, but unrecognized.

I always want to complicate everything; it is how I keep things interesting and compelling. And while it may be indicative of the art of being a Christian—an art espoused by painters, sculptors, musicians, liturgists and all other "complicators" of the worship of God—the danger is letting the complication get in the way of the faith. To be a Christian is to believe in God and to have faith in the salvation offered by that belief. Everything else is an aid to faith. I am not despising all the aesthetic complications of worship; on the contrary, as a Catholic I revel in them. I consider the complications of worship necessary for my individual ongoing process of relating to God. I acknowledge, however, that these complications can all too often separate me from what is important. If the ritual does not go well then I am disappointed and miss the meaning of the worship. More gravely, there was a time when I let the negative theological complication of homophobia stand between God and me.

Today I am faced with the question of how to use all the various aids to faith—the church service, daily readings, the saints, the liturgy of the hours—effectively as tools to bring me closer to God. The point of these aids is to use them to see Jesus' presence everyday, everywhere. Each day I read the Psalms that are recited worldwide, and have been throughout history, by people who were also looking

for and found God. In this way, I individually and collectively daily
worship God. This ongoing liturgical witness is the window through
which I can see Christ.

SILENCE

PRAYER

Gracious God, do not let me be blinded by ritual
but instead let it be the periscope through which I see Christ.

January 3

PSALM

Let the sea roar, and all that fills it;
the world and those who live in it.
Let the floods clap their hands;
let the hills sing together for joy
at the presence of the Lord.
(Ps 98:7–9a)

SCRIPTURE

1 John 2:29—3:6; Psalm 98:1, 3–6; John 1:29–34

MEDITATION

John's two themes are faith and love and this epistle reading is an
elaboration of those themes. In today's readings John talks about the
effect faith and love have in our life. In today's Gospel the Baptist is
the witness that Jesus is the Son of God.

On one hand I like the idea that Christian faith means that no one
who remains in Christ sins (see 1 Jn 3:6). That means that from the
viewpoint of pain I should now be free, and that I am in a superior
position to non-believers who are still in their sins. While I have heard
many Christians imply this superior condition, I have not really seen it
as a reality in either their lives or my own. It makes me wonder how
this is supposed to work.

I recognize that there have been moments in my life when I have
been a perfected Christian, when I have responded out of love.

Invariably I see those moments in hindsight when someone else tells me how I had a positive impact on him or her in some way that I had not conciously intended. Those are the moments when I am God's instrument of peace to another person. Often when I purposely try to be perfect I fail. How can I be perfected (made whole) when the feeling I have is one of superiority rather than love?

I have come to believe that the best effort I make toward Christian perfection is that of pre-disposition, making myself as available as possible to be an instrument of God's peace. Generally this means that I do not seek opportunities to tell people what is wrong with them and what they need to do to fix themselves. Instead I try to fathom my own failings, bring them to God for forgiveness or redemption, and be available if God sees fit to recommend me to somebody in need.

SILENCE

PRAYER

God, help me to be consoling, loving, and understanding and not so preening, demanding, and pedantic.

January 4

PSALM

Make a joyful noise to the Lord, all the earth...
make a joyful noise before the Sovereign, the Lord.
(Ps 98: 4a, 6b)

SCRIPTURE

1 John 3:7–10; Psalm 98:1, 7–9; John 1:35–42

MEDITATION

Since January 2 the daily readings have been from St. John who has been elaborating the themes of faith and love and giving witness to Jesus in the Gospel. Today another witness to Jesus, Andrew, introduces Simon Peter whom Jesus renames "the Rock." The good news is spreading.

Ultimately, as we know, Peter not only gets a nickname, he is traditionally understood to be the foundation upon which Jesus builds the church. Additionally, we discover that Peter has feet of clay—much in the same way that King David was less than perfect in his relationship with God. And yet, Peter is the original "Rock." As we have seen, John's message is fairly straightforward: believe and love. And when we believe, love, and make ourselves available to God, then we too form a part of the foundation for the spread of the good news.

It is not that I have to be perfect in my adherence to a set of rules devised by myself or others. Nor is it that I always have to be strong enough to overcome sin each time it enters my life. It is that I need to recognize God's love for me and the whole creation and stay involved in the process of growing through faith. When I do that I too am a bearer of the good news.

SILENCE

PRAYER

God, forgive me for my sins
and use me for your good works.

January 5

PSALM

Know that the Lord is God.
It is God that made us, and we are God's.
(Ps 100:3a)

SCRIPTURE

1 John 3:11–21; Psalm 100:1–5; John 1:43–51

MEDITATION

John's witness to Jesus and the good news continues in today's Gospel as Jesus calls Philip and Nathaniel to be his disciples. The Epistle exhorts us to love our sisters and brothers.

How shall we express our faithfulness and our love? Sometimes I find loving others exhausting. I am not a naturally gregarious or outgoing person. Social interaction wears me out quickly, especially when I encounter people I do not know. The time it takes to become involved with new people is draining to me. I am usually really talkative only when I am with my close friends. When I was younger I thought that being outgoing was a choice and that something was wrong with me for not choosing to be more outgoing. I thought that my introversion was part of a self-inflicted repression. When I came out I thought that being openly gay would make me more outgoing (I even hoped that coming out would make me able to dance better). But the truth is that I am an introvert and stereotypes of gregarious gay men could not help me become something that I am not. But John's message today is not "become more outgoing," it is have faith and show love.

Although I make myself available to others when appropriate—such as when they ask for help—I no longer feel distressed at my quiet, inward nature. One effective tool that I have for loving others is prayer. I can pray for others every day, light candles for them, and remember them in their needs.

SILENCE

PRAYER

Gracious God, I pray for my friends, my family, my co-workers, and all those whom I encounter today.

January 6

This is the reading when Epiphany is celebrated on the second Sunday after Christmas day and January 6 falls prior to Epiphany.

PSALM

God's delight is not in the strength of the horse,
nor pleasure in the speed of the runner;

but the Lord takes pleasure in those who fear God,
in those who hope in God's steadfast love.
(Ps 147:10–11)

SCRIPTURE

1 John 5:5–13; Psalm 147:12–15, 19–20; Mark 1:7–11

MEDITATION

We finish the week with John's continuing exhortations to faith and
with the witness of St. Mark about Jesus.

I sometimes wonder what it means for me to witness to Jesus
Christ. When I talk about Christian faith there are times when I feel
a little Pollyannaish. The Christian message all sounds good in theo-
ry—and so do I—but the messy reality of my life does not always
match my grand theological understandings. I have seen Christ proclaimed by sidewalk preachers with bullhorns and I cringe at the idea
that witnessing to Christ means doing something similar. When I feel
nervous about speaking as a person of faith I ask myself if I am just a
coward or is my faith a weak faith. Do I really believe all this stuff?
Am I scared to stand up for what I believe even with other gay people? Am I afraid to speak when being a Christian sounds a little
embarrassing?

Today's Scripture helps me realize that faith means being willing to
be an instrument of God. And just as I would not use a lawn mower
to trim bushes, God is not going to misuse me as an instrument of
the good news. If I relax and just be myself then God's message of
love will be transmitted to those who find a person like me a suitable
channel for hearing the good news. My witness is in being honest
about myself—it is not in trying to make myself over into something
that I am not.

SILENCE

PRAYER

God, I pray that I may be your effective tool,
whether it is to sow love, pardon, faith, hope, light, or joy.

Sunday in the Octave of Christmas, Feast of the Holy Family

This meditation takes the place of whichever dated January meditation falls on the first Sunday after Christmas Day.

PSALM

Happy is everyone who fears the Lord,
who walks in God's ways.
You shall eat the fruit of the labor of your hands;
you shall be happy, and it shall go well with you.
(Ps 128:1–2)

SCRIPTURE

Sirach 3:2–6, 12–14; Psalm 128:1–5; Colossians 3:12–21

Gospel

Year A:
Matthew 2:13–15, 19–23;
Year B:
Luke 2:22–40;
Year C:
Luke 2:41–52

MEDITATION

In commemorating the Holy Family of Jesus, his mother Mary and St. Joseph, we value our own families as well. We remember our parents and siblings and pray for them whether or not our day-to-day relationships with them are positive.

On this day I also remember my extended family, or "family of choice." These are the people who are not related to me but who occupy positions of love and trust in my life. These are the people whom I have come to know and respect because of their love and honesty with me. I give thanks especially for all my straight friends who embraced me with love and acceptance when I came out of the closet. And I pray for those few friends and family members who did not and do not embrace me now.

SILENCE

PRAYER

As Saint Joseph prayed for his wife and child,
I pray for my friends and family as well,
that we too may be a holy people for God.

Solemnity of the Epiphany of the Lord

PSALM

For God delivers the needy when they call,
the poor and those who have no helper.
From oppression and violence God redeems their life;
and precious is their blood in God's sight.
(Ps 72:12, 14)

SCRIPTURE

Isaiah 60:1–6; Psalm 72:1–2, 7-8, 10–13; Ephesians 3:2–3a, 5-6;
Matthew 2:1–12

MEDITATION

This is the Twelfth Day of Christmas, the traditional end to the
Christmas season. Throughout the last days the readings have been
witnessing to Christ and his message and on this day we celebrate the
"manifestation" of our Lord. This is really the topic of the whole season from the incarnation when Jesus is made humanly present to
today when the visit of the Magi makes Christ known to the whole
world.

On this day I remember that Christ is also born within me, and as
such, I make Jesus manifest to the world as well. With all my faults,
gifts, peculiarities, talents, idiosyncrasies and my same-sex orientation,
I am a proclamation of the love and the will of God. Denying Jesus,
denying being gay or lesbian, denying our nature is a denial of God.
Instead of denial I will seek continually to affirm who I am. My
heartfelt desire is to know the will of God for love in my life and to
have the strength to make that love manifest, to follow it through.

SILENCE

PRAYER

Wondrous God, through prayer and meditation
I seek constant contact with you,
grant me the strength to follow your will for me.

PART THREE

Advent Group Study Guide

SMALL GROUP STUDY GUIDELINES

An effective small group study series will agree on certain objectives and procedures before it begins. The following are some recommended guidelines to help the group get started.

Purpose

Be clear about your purpose. Ask the participants to name their reasons for getting together for the Advent and Christmas season. You may hear such answers as to learn, to deepen faith, to explore new ideas, for friendship. Each answer is a "right" answer and will help the group shape a common purpose.

Time and Place

As a group agree on how many weeks the sessions will last. This book outlines four sessions, but the material can certainly be reworked to include fewer or more sessions, depending upon the group's interests. Together select a specific meeting day, meeting place, and beginning and ending times. I recommend 60 to 90 minutes for each session.

Preparation

Together agree on what homework the group expects of each participant. In my experience discussions proceed most meaningfully when participants have read the Gospel passage and the commentary before arriving.

Ground Rules

Religion, like politics, can get under everybody's skin. For that reason it is a good idea to allow room for questions and to create a safe place for people to challenge central issues of the faith. At times that may mean holding your tongue and allowing the Holy Spirit to function through the group. Before you begin create a set of two or three ground rules that will guide your time together. Ground rules may include such statements as: We will speak honestly and share our true thoughts and feelings. We will listen to one another with respect. We will take turns and encourage everyone to speak.

Because small groups often bond quickly you may also want to decide whether or not new people can be admitted to the group once it starts.

Leadership

Decide whether you will have one group leader, a different leader each week with responsibility for facilitating the discussion, or perhaps no specified leader. You may also want to decide if there should be a host for each session to make sure that the meeting place is set up and any amenities are prepared.

Process

When everyone has arrived and greeted one another, begin with a simple prayer and then read the gospel aloud to the group.

Discuss the questions that are provided. There may be more questions than you can address during each session. Select those that seem most important for the needs and interests of your group.

WEEK 1 (ON OR AFTER THE FIRST SUNDAY IN ADVENT): THE SECOND COMING

Read the appropriate texts depending on whether it is year A, B, or C. See "Reading Cycle for Advent and Christmas" (pp. 99–106). Notice what word or phrase holds your attention.

Gospel Readings

Catholic Lectionary	Revised Common Lectionary
Year A:	Year A:
Matthew 24:37–44	Matthew 24:36–44
Year B:	Year B:
Mark 13:33–37	Mark 13:24–37
Year C:	Year C:
Luke 21:25–28, 34–36	Luke 21:25–36

Gospel Commentary

There will be signs of its approach, but we will not know when the Second Coming will happen. Jesus admonished his listeners always to be prepared. Preparation is our task. We are in a process of becoming ready. And even though there may be some pain or discomfort, there is always the joyful knowledge of that for which we are preparing, the return of the Son of Man.

DEFINING THE SECOND COMING

We declare in the Nicene Creed that Jesus will, ". . . come again in glory to judge the living and the dead," and the reign Jesus heralds will have no end. This Second Coming is to be the culmination of history and the saving work begun by Christ.

The question is: What significance will this have for our life today? If the reign of God is always at hand, and redemption has already been achieved, what are we waiting for? Largely, I think, we are waiting for our own development as individuals to be complete and we are waiting to integrate ourselves into the larger community of which we have always been a part.

Christian faith is not a solitary activity. While we have a responsibility to work out our lives individually, we do so within the context of a community. And as we seek to perfect ourselves, our community is assisting us, and in return we help our community reach its perfection, its wholeness. This is our transaction in the economy of salvation, and it is a perpetual transaction. Its conclusion lies in God's will. Our responsibility is to be involved with people and ourselves in a positive, faithful way.

Questions for Discussion

1. What word or phrase caught your attention as the Gospel was read today? What do you think that word or phrase is saying to you today?

2. How do you feel about your psychological, emotional, and physical care of yourself? What is causing you to feel that way? How do you think taking care of yourself relates to today's Gospel reading?

3. How are you feeling about your relationship with God? What is causing you to feel that way? What does your relationship with God have to do with today's Gospel reading?

4. How do you feel about your family? Your friends? The gay or lesbian community? The North American community? The world community?

5. What does the community of saints mean to you? Do you feel you have community with them? What would or does community with them look like?

6. How do you use community (family, friends, the gay or lesbian community, the church, the saints who have gone before you) to develop your spiritual life? How does relationship with community relate to today's Gospel reading?

7. How do you contribute to your community's ability to help others? What do you do to enact social justice? What does helping others and enacting justice have to do with today's Gospel reading?

8. If God called you home right now would you be ready? Why or why not?

9. What did you hear in today's discussion that will help you as you seek to become more whole, both as an individual and as a community?

WEEK 2 (ON OR AFTER THE SECOND SUNDAY IN ADVENT): PENITENTIAL HOUSE CLEANING

Read the appropriate texts depending on whether it is year A, B, or C. See "Reading Cycle for Advent and Christmas" (pp. 99–106). Notice what word or phrase holds your attention.

Gospel Reading

Catholic Lectionary	Revised Common Lectionary
Year A:	Year A:
Mathew 3:1–12	Matthew 3:1–12
Year B:	Year B:
Mark 1:1–8	Mark 1:1–8
Year C:	Year C:
Luke 3:1–6	Luke 3:1–6

Gospel Commentary

The Gospel readings for this second Sunday in Advent focus on John the Baptist and his call for preparation for the coming of the Lord. The holidays are often a time for visiting and frequently we clean our homes to prepare for the arrival of family and friends. As we joyfully await the birth of Jesus we can respond to John's call for preparation and do some penitential work in advance of Jesus' arrival.

DEFINING PENANCE

In the Gospel reading John calls for repentance. The term penance comes from the Latin *paenitentia* and means "repentance." Traditionally, the Catholic Church has taught that repentance permits us to recognize our sins and return to God through contrition. Repentence means to "turn around." In the Protestant church repentance and confession is most frequently practiced as a corporate act during worship. In the Catholic Church the traditional penitential activity for Advent is the Examination of Conscience and the Sacrament of Reconciliation (or what we used to call confession). In addition, during Advent some Catholics and Protestants undertake certain penitential activities like daily confession, fasting, or abstinence as ways to remind them of their desire to "turn around."

St. James writes, "Therefore confess your sins to one another, and pray for one another that you may be healed. The prayer of the righteous is powerful and effective" (Jas 5:16). While many Christians understandably object to the idea that a mere human has the capacity to forgive sins, there is a profoundly therapeutic value to unburdening oneself with another person. This has been shown to be effective in both standard therapeutic care and in the substance abuse recovery movement. Forgiveness comes from God but God often uses another human being to carry the message of forgiveness to us by hearing what we have to say and helping us to put our confession into perspective.

WHY REPENT?

While we may be different from the majority in who we fall in love with, we are not different in the difficulties that confound our lives. While being who we are, or being in a loving, same-sex relationship, is not sinful, there are experiences of sin that we each need to examine—just like straight people. As gay and lesbian people we have so often been unjustly condemned that any religiously-based examination of sin risks being offensive. However, I invite you into a discussion to explore the concepts of sin and redemption as you experience them, and to do so in a positive, healthy and affirming manner.

Questions for Discussion

1. What word or phrase caught your attention as the Gospel passage was read today? What do you think that word or phrase is saying to you today?

2. Does your church offer a formal ritual for confession? Is it private or corporate? What difference do you see in the effectiveness of a corporate ritual for confession over a private ritual of confession? A private ritual over a corporate ritual?

3. What do you think about confessing your sins to another person? Have you ever done so? If so, share the story and how it made you feel. If not, what prevents you from doing so?

4. As a Christian what value do you see in penitential activities like daily confession, fasting, prayer, or abstinence? If you practice penitential activities how do the activities function in your spiritual development?

5. What activities do you do to prepare during Advent? How do they contribute to your preparation for Jesus birth?

WEEK 3 (ON OR AFTER THE THIRD SUNDAY IN ADVENT): JOYFUL EXPECTATION

Read the appropriate texts depending on whether it is year A, B, or C. See "Reading Cycle for Advent and Christmas" (pp. 99–106).

Gospel Readings

Catholic Lectionary	Revised Common Lectionary
Year A:	**Year A:**
Matthew 11:2–11	Matthew 11:2–11
Year B:	**Year B:**
John 1:6–8, 19–28	John 1:6–8, 19–28
Year C:	**Year C:**
Luke 3:10–18	Luke 3:7–18

Gospel Commentary

John is preparing the way for Jesus and announcing the approach of the good news. John is questioned about his witness, if indeed he is the messiah. John points out that there is one greater than he coming.

In Matthew we hear that in Jesus' ministry the blind receive their sight, the lame walk, the lepers are cleansed, the deaf hear, the dead are raised, and the poor have good news brought to them. In Luke we hear John the Baptist announce that whoever has two coats must share one with someone who has none and soldiers should not extort money from anyone by false accusation.

In the first chapter of John we are assured that Jesus is the one we have been waiting for, the one who will fulfill the expectations of all.

DEFINING JOYFUL EXPECTATION

We are all waiting, waiting to have our own deafness cured, waiting to receive a coat that we need, waiting to be spiritually raised from the dead. Advent is a time of joyful expectation because we hear again that God loves us so profoundly that God comes to live in the world with us. The consolation of religion, especially as it has been offered to gay and lesbian people, may seem ephemeral at best, cruel at worst. However, the promise of Christian faith seems to be a happier human condition, even for us! In the "Brief Order for Confession and Forgiveness" used by the Lutheran church, we acknowledge our sinfulness and plead with God for mercy. The expectation is that we shall be forgiven, renewed, and led so that as we say to God, "we may delight in your will and walk in your ways, to the glory of our holy name" (*Lutheran Book of Worship*, p. 56). Advent is a good time to begin exploring just what the delight is in following the will of God. Advent is a good time to remember the joy of being fully embraced and loved by God.

Questions for Discussion

1. What word or phrase caught your attention as the Gospel was read today? What do you think that word or phrase is saying to you today?

2. As a gay or lesbian Christian, what are you daily waiting for?

3. As a Christian what expectations do you have? How does that expectation square with your same-sex attraction?

4. For you, what joyfulness is there in being a Christian? How do you describe Christian faith from your viewpoint?

5. As a Christian, how do you balance the fulfillment of your needs with your wants?

6. What are traditional Christian sexual ethics? What value do you see in that traditional model of sexual ethics?

7. Do gay and lesbian people have a different sexual ethic? How does it compare to a straight sexual ethic?

8. If you were to compose a gay or lesbian statement of Christian love what would you say? How would your sexual ethic manifest itself in that statement?

WEEK 4 (ON OR AFTER THE CELEBRATION OF CHRISTMAS—BEFORE JANUARY 6): INCARNATE LOVE

Read one or all of the gospel accounts of Jesus' birth.

Gospel Readings

Matthew 1:1–25; Luke 2:1–20; John 1:1–18

Gospel Commentary

Christ is born. God has become incarnate as a sure sign of the love of God. God has not come to us as a powerful king, or a mighty warrior, or a Hollywood action hero. God has come as a weak and vulnerable child, born in a barn with animals. God enters our history on the margins, and it is those on the margins—poor agricultural workers on the night shift—who are the first witnesses to this wonder.

DEFINING THE INCARNATION

According to the *Catholic Encyclopedia* incarnation "is the assumption of human nature, including human body, human soul and will, and all human characteristics except sin, by God the Son" (p. 289). The *Oxford Companion to the Bible* states that the "dualism of flesh and spirit and its overcoming in the incarnation . . . held that the goal of the incarnation was the transformation of the human into a nature compatible with the divine" (p. 301). It says further that "some regard incarnation as an ancient mythological form of thought; others see in the incarnation a clue to the universal entering of God into human life; still others see the particularity of the incarnation in Jesus Christ as the distinctive core of Christianity" (p. 301).

God has become human in order to save us both through the redemption offered by Christ on the cross and through the moral agency of Jesus' human example on earth. We find modeled in the life of Jesus in the Gospels a way for us to live out the fullness of God's gift of human life. We too are incarnate love. And we too have a ministry to live out on earth as an example of what that love means.

Questions for Discussion

1. What word or phrase caught your attention as the Gospel was read today? What do you think that word or phrase is saying to you today?

2. In your understanding is Christ's incarnation a mythological understanding, a historical reality, or both? What does the incarnation mean to you?

3. What difference is there between humility and humiliation? How do you participate in those two different conditions?

4. How is same-sex love incarnate love?

5. If you too are an incarnation of God's love, how does that knowledge influence your life?

PART FOUR

Individual Practices for Advent

MORNING AND EVENING PRAYER

Morning and Evening Prayer are the hinges of daily prayer, known traditionally as the "divine office" or the "liturgy of the hours." The liturgy of the hours dates back to the apostolic exhortation to pray constantly and derives from the Jewish practice of daily prayer at specific times of the day. The traditional hours for prayer were Lauds, just before dawn; Prime, about 6 a.m.; Terce, about 9 a.m.; Sext, at noon; None, about 3 p.m.; Vespers, evening prayer, at dusk; Compline, prayed just before bedtime; Matins, prayed sometime after midnight, usually between 3 and 4 a.m. This remained the traditional arrangement of the hours until the 1960s. At that time a wider emphasis on all Christians praying the "divine office" was encouraged. The number of hours was reduced by one, and Matins was modified so that it could be recited at any other hour of the day.

The centerpiece of the "divine office" is the book of Psalms. The 150 psalms are the prayer book of the church. Begin your morning and your evening prayer by reading one of the Psalms indicated.

MORNING PRAYER

Upon rising, find a quiet place to pray.

Read one of the following psalms:

5, 8, 19, 24, 29, 33, 36, 42, 43, 47, 48, 51, 57, 63, 65, 67, 77, 80, 81, 84-87, 90, 92, 93, 96–101, 108, 117–119, 135, 143, 144, 146–150.

Reflect on the morning Antiphon for the week.

WEEK 1: God is my protection, my wall and defense; let the gates open for God is with me.

WEEK 2: I declare to the ends of the world: God has done marvelous things for me.

WEEK 3: I am the Holy One of Israel. I will be with you, says the Lord.

WEEK 4: Watch, wait and have patience. For the Lord God draws near.

Read and reflect on the lectionary reading for the day.
See "Reading Cycle for Advent and Christmas" (pages 99–106).

Pray this or another prayer of your heart.

WEEKS 1 & 2: When my soul is cast down, yet will I praise you God. Strengthen me in your will.

WEEKS 3 & 4: You desire truth in my inward being, God; therefore teach me wisdom in my heart.

Recite the Canticle of Zechariah (Lk 1:67–79)

Blessed be the Lord God of Israel,
for God has looked favorably on the people
and redeemed them.
God has raised up a mighty savior for us
in the house of God's servant David,
as God spoke through the mouth
of the holy prophets from of old,
that we would be saved from our enemies
and from the hand of all who hate us.
Thus God has shown the mercy promised to our ancestors,
and has remembered the holy covenant,
the oath that God swore to our ancestor Abraham,
to grant us that we, being rescued from the hands of our enemies,
might serve the Lord without fear, in holiness and righteousness
before God all our days.
And you, child, will be called
the prophet of the Most High;

for you will go before the Lord
to prepare the way,
to give knowledge of salvation to God's people
by the forgiveness of their sins.
By the tender mercy of our God,
the dawn from on high will break upon us,
to give light to those who sit in darkness
and in the shadow of death,
to guide our feet into the way of peace.

EVENING PRAYER

Before retiring find a quiet place to pray.

Read one of the following psalms:

11, 15, 16, 20, 21, 27, 30, 32, 41, 45, 46, 49, 62, 67, 72, 110–116, 119, 121–124, 126, 130–132, 135–139, 141, 142, 144, 145.

Reflect on the Antiphon for the week.

WEEK 1: To you, O Lord, I lift up, I lift up my soul to you.

WEEK 2: Bless us, O Lord, as we await your coming.

WEEK 3: Come to us, O Lord, and give us peace in your companionship.

WEEK 4: O Sacred God of ancient Israel, stretch out your mighty hand to save us.

Pray this or another prayer of your heart.

WEEKS 1 & 2: Gracious God, I pray for peace, I pray for justice, I pray for mercy, I pray for all those who have no one to pray for them.

WEEKS 3 & 4: Holy God, protect me as I stay awake, watch over me as I sleep, that awake, I may watch with Christ, and asleep, rest in his peace. Send peaceful sleep, O God, to restore my body and mind. I ask this through Christ our Lord.

Recite the Magnificat (Lk 1:46–55):

My soul magnifies the Lord,
and my spirit rejoices in God my Savior,
for God has looked with favor on the lowliness of this servant.
Surely, from now on all generations will call me blessed;
for the Mighty One has done great things for me,
and holy is God's name.
The Lord's mercy is for those who fear God
from generation to generation.
God has shown strength with God's arm;
God has scattered the proud in the thoughts of their hearts.
God has brought down the powerful from their thrones,
and lifted up the lowly;
God has filled the hungry with good things,
and sent the rich away empty.
God has helped God's servant Israel,
in remembrance of mercy,
according to the promise God made to our ancestors,
to Abraham and to his descendants forever.

EXAMINATION OF CONSCIENCE

An "examination of conscience" is traditionally a part of the confession of sins, which is a practice particularly associated with the Catholic faith. However, Anglican and Protestant traditions maintain it as well. The *Lutheran Book of Worship* contains both a corporate rite for Sundays in the "Brief Order for Confession and Forgiveness" and the rite of "Individual Confession and Forgiveness."

Many people today continue to be suspicious of confession and reject the notion that one individual can absolve another from sin. And yet at the same time the value of personal examination and psychological unburdening has become widespread through various forms of therapy. Outside the church in both standard psychological counseling and in the movement for recovery from substance abuse the value of talking to someone about the nature of one's past actions—right and wrong—has been affirmed. Since the 1970s, in churches where confession is commonly practiced, an emphasis on dealing with actions and circumstances that distanced one from communion with God and with community has emerged as the focus. Advent is not a penitential season. Lent is the traditional season of repentance. However, an examination of conscience is a helpful way to reflect during this period of joyful expectation.

When he came, Jesus revealed God to us. Jesus, through his humanity, also reveals us to ourselves, and in the conclusion to the Sermon on the Mount he says, "Be perfect, therefore, as your heavenly Father is perfect" (Mt 5:48). Catholic Bishop Thomas Gumbleton wrote an essay entitled "A Call to Listen: The Church's Pastoral and Theological Response to Gays and Lesbians," published in *Sexual Diversity and Catholicism*. In it he states that " . . . just as God is fully and completely God in the fullness of what it means to be God, so each of us is called by God to be fully and completely the human person God has made us to be . . . homosexual persons can be 'perfect,' just as heterosexual persons can be" (pp. 3–4). Bishop Gumbleton adds that "homosexual persons must struggle to reach as full a human development as possible by using the same resources of guidance God has given for all" (p. 4). An "examination of conscience" is one such resource available to gay men and lesbian women in achieving the fullness of who we are.

This section will explore an approach to an examination of conscience based on the Ten Commandments. The version I include here has been slightly modified in order to reflect those who experience same-sex love.

Christian Examination of Conscience

Traditionally the confession of sins frees us and facilitates our reconciliation with others. Through this practice we look squarely at our sins, take responsibility for them, and open ourselves to God and to communion with the church and the rest of the world. This practice has not only a personal benefit, but a communal one as well. On a personal level, this practice helps us reconnect to God's grace in an intimate friendship. Reconciliation with God is the effect of self-examination. From a communal viewpoint it reconciles the individual with the church and the world as a whole. Not only is the individual healed, but his or her healing restores health to the whole community.

How to Practice Christian Examination of Conscience

The following outlines the process of Christian self-examination. I share it with you here as a resource for your Advent practice. I suggest you begin with a simple preparatory prayer and then ask yourself the questions that follow it. Be gentle with yourself. This is not an exercise to "catch you" doing something wrong but rather to bring your full attention to your God-given life.

Read through the questions slowly. Give yourself time to reflect. You may want to reflect on only one commandment per day or you may want to use the Christian Examination of Conscience only once at the beginning of the season of Advent.

PREPARATORY PRAYER

Creator God, Enlightenment of the World, give me the courage, strength, and love to see myself fully, the good and the bad, and take responsibility for my actions right and wrong. I pray that I may be honest, straightforward and offer a contrite heart.

PREPARATORY QUESTIONS

1. How long has it been since my last examination of conscience?

2. Did I discuss the issues raised by that examination with anyone? If not, would that have helped? Will it help now?

3. Did I take any necessary actions that I discerned needed to be done?

4. Did I hide anything at that time that needs to be brought to light now?

EXAMINATION OF CONSCIENCE USING THE TEN COMMANDMENTS

Protestant and Catholic traditions use slightly different wording and numbering of the Ten Commandments. I have used the Catholic tradition in order to highlight the relationship that exists between two committed people, instead of demoting it to the level of a material object.

One: I am your God, you shall not have false gods before me.

Have I allowed idols—work, power, money, material objects, my body, sex—to become the center of my life? Have I rejected God in my life? Have I despaired of God's help? Do I allow superstition— horoscopes, tarot, chance—more decision-making power than prayerful discernment of God's will? How have I honored God in my life?

Two: You shall not take the name of God in vain.

Have I called upon God's help falsely? Have I made promises to God or others with no intention of living up to what I have said? How have I affirmatively proclaimed God's name?

Three: You shall keep the Sabbath day holy.

Have I recognized the importance of a day of rest? Do I use the day of rest for work, household chores, activities that do not lead to my physical, emotional and psychological re-creation? Do I regularly participate in communal worship of God? What do I do to honor God and myself?

Four: You shall honor your father and mother.

Have I acknowledged my parents appropriately? Even if faced with their disapproval have I insured that my behavior towards them demonstrates respect for giving me life? How can I show them respect if they have none for me? Do I show respect for legitimate authority in my life? What is appropriate authority in my life, and how do I respect it?

Five: You shall not kill.

Have I indulged in behavior that is self-destructive or dangerous for others? Have I hurt anyone's reputation? Have I wished bad things for others? Have I conducted myself in a way that could lead others to self-destructive behavior? How can I make a positive statement for life in my community?

Six: You shall not commit adultery.

Have I abused the gift of my sexuality? Have I abused others through sex? Have I cheated on any commitments involving the gift of sexuality? How do I see sexual activity as a positive aspect of my life?

Seven: You shall not steal.

Have I stolen? Have I stolen time from my employer? Have I denied my colleagues just compensation of either time or money? Have I taken credit for other's ideas? When I feel denied, am I tempted to find a short cut to what I want? How can that sense of denial be an asset in my life?

Eight: You shall not bear false witness against your neighbor.

Have I lied? Have I gossiped about another person? Have I revealed confidences? Have I used friends, family members, or colleagues for my own advantage? How have I affirmed rather than derided those around me?

Nine: You shall not covet your neighbor's spouse.

Have I indulged in inappropriate behavior towards someone else's spouse or partner? Have I felt inferior because of the love a friend receives from someone significant in his or her life? If I feel lacking in intimate love in my life what opportunity does that present for deepening my relationship with God?

Ten: You shall not covet your neighbor's goods.

Do I experience jealousy because of someone else's looks, or job, or material objects? Do I allow a sense of competition with others to govern my life? Am I more concerned with my appearance, or my home, or my job than in my relationship with God? What can I do to distinguish between what it is that I need from what it is that I want?

What Next?

Once an examination of conscience has been completed the question is what to do with it. While you may now have a better grasp of the emotional terrain you are on, one serious risk is misunderstanding the value of what has been discovered. The bad may be overblown while the good is underplayed. Another form of arrogance is thinking that you are worse than you really are. Talking things over with another person helps to put the issues into perspective.

The traditional Christian understanding of confession is that it helps us in conscience formation and heals us as we progress in the life of the Spirit. Through regular self-examination and unburdening we receive the gift of God's mercy and we are more able to be merciful as God is merciful. Christian examination of conscience is a path to a healthy humility and the experience of joy about who you are, an incarnate sign of God's love. This Advent season remember that Jesus is born daily. God comes and God abides.

PART FIVE

Family and/or Group Practices for Advent

Throughout the Christian faith there are a variety of ways of commemorating the Advent Season from calendars and candles to cookies and cards. Symbols and ritual actions are the ways in which people internalize important events of their lives to make them meaningful. Gay and lesbian people have not always identified with Christian symbols because they have been created around concepts of family that were then used to make us feel unwelcome. The communal and familial values, and the rituals that attend them, are important for the emotional and physical well-being of the individual, including our well-being. That is why using symbolic activities in the major Christian seasons, in conjunction with a network of supportive friends and family, is important for us as believers as well.

For gay men and lesbian women the concept of family can be broader than the norm for heterosexuals. On the positive side, we can be fully accepted and affirmed by our biological families and fully participatory in major Christian events with them. In other cases we need to develop a "family of choice" distinct from our "family of origin" in order to make the kind of social and communal connections which aid in the development of Christian faith.

The Advent season generally lasts three full weeks and some portion of a fourth week. The goal of this section is to offer an Advent practice that could be adopted by a family or friendship group. The point here is not to state the best way to commemorate the season, but to highlight the importance of symbolic and communal action and provide a model for it.

THE FIRST SUNDAY OF ADVENT: THE ADVENT WREATH

The Advent wreath is a circle of evergreen branches that contains four candles, which are lit at the beginning of each of the four weeks of Advent.

Traditionally three of the candles are purple or blue and one is pink. The pink candle is lit on the third Sunday of Advent (known as "Gaudete" or "Rejoice Sunday"). The origins of the Advent wreath are uncertain. It may be related to the ancient practice of wreaths as adornment or it may be an ancient symbol for victory. Another possible source is the "crown of lights" worn by Swedish girls on the feast of St. Lucia.

Activity

Prepare an Advent wreath and set it out on the primary dining table in your home so that it will be visible during meal times throughout the weeks ahead. During the evening meal on the first Sunday of Advent light the first blue or purple candle. Read the following Scripture and pray the Advent prayer:

> Be alert at all times, praying that you may have the strength to escape all these things that will take place, and to stand before the Son of Man (Lk 21:36).

> Gracious God, bless our Advent wreath. Be with us as we began our preparation for the coming of the Savior. As we light a candle every day, help us to stay constant and burning brightly in your love. Amen.

Invite the persons at the table to tell stories from their day that reminds them that the light of God is dawning and growing stronger in the world. Pray the prayer every evening this week as the first candle is lit for the evening meal.

THE SECOND SUNDAY OF ADVENT: THE CRÈCHE

Until the fourth week of Advent place the empty manger in a prominent position in the main room of the house. Let the vacant structure help you anticipate the joy that is to come, and remind you of the penitential housecleaning that is a part of the season.

A crèche is a traditional "manger scene." The word is from the French. Manger scenes as a symbol of the season are very old. Beginning in 1223 St. Francis of Assisi popularized their use by the laity when he used live animals and people as a part of a worship service. The traditional manger scene is normally composed of animal figures (donkey, cattle, and sheep), human figures of shepherds and the Magi (or three wise men), and the Holy Family of St. Joseph, the Blessed Virgin Mary, and the infant Jesus. Usually the scene is centered within a barn-like structure that may be surmounted by a star, an angel, or both.

Activity

Place the animals in the crèche: the donkey, cattle, sheep or any others. The primary purpose of the manger was as a feeding place for domestic animals. Let their presence during the following week be a reminder of the humility in which Christ was born.

During the evening meal on the second Sunday of Advent light the first and second blue or purple candles. Read the following Scripture and pray the Advent prayer.

As it is written in the book of the words of the prophet Isaiah,
"The voice of one crying out in the wilderness:
'Prepare the way of the Lord,
make the paths straight . . .
and all the flesh shall see the salvation of God'" (Lk 3:4, 6).

Holy God, who is ever present to us, remind of us your constant love. Make us an instrument of your will so that the gifts you have given us may serve to do good to others. Keep us alert to your will and be with us as we wait the coming of the Savior. Amen.

Invite the persons at the table to tell stories from their life that reminds them how God shelters and feeds the whole creation, including them. Pray the prayer every evening this week as the first and second candles are lit for the evening meal.

THE THIRD SUNDAY OF ADVENT: THE CHRISTMAS TREE

The third Sunday is "Gaudete" or "Rejoice Sunday." It is a day of special rejoicing as we are now more than halfway through the wait. A good way

to mark the joyful nature of this day is to set up a Christmas tree.
Once again, the origins of this symbol are obscure. There is a tradition
that St. Boniface (c. 675–754 AD) is the source of the decorated tree, perhaps due to his appropriation of a sacred oak tree at Geismar during his
evangelization of the Germans. Another tradition attributes the tree to
Martin Luther. It certainly appears to have been a tradition that arose in
Germany, where it is known as the *tannenbaum*. The Christmas tree was
popularized in the United States in the nineteenth century when German
immigrants brought it to Pennsylvania. Prince Albert, the German consort
to Queen Victoria, also promoted its use, and it became part of the
Victorian theme of Christmas commonly portrayed today.

Originally apples—a symbol of the fall of Adam—were used to decorate the tree; later wafers, representing the Eucharist and salvation, were
added. These eventually were transformed into pastry decorations of
angels, bells, and other objects until ultimately they became the modern
Christmas decorations. The first lights on the tree were candles meant to
represent Christ as the light of the world. In one tradition, on Christmas
Eve parents would decorate the Christmas tree and then the children
would be awoken just after midnight to find the tree decorated and presents underneath.

Activity

Place the shepherds in the crèche. These simple and humble working men
and women received a divine message from the angel and were the first to
witness the coming of Christ. Throughout the week let their presence be
a reminder that it is the least who will be first in the realm of God. At this
time place the figures of the Magi in some other part of the room, showing that they too are on the way to witness the coming of Immanuel, God
with us.

During the evening meal on the third Sunday of Advent light the first
and second blue or purple candle and then light the pink candle. Read the
following Scripture and pray the Advent prayer.

As the people were filled with expectation, and all were questioning in their
hearts concerning John, whether he might be the Messiah, John answered all

of them by saying, "I baptize you with water; but one who is more powerful than I is coming" (Lk 3:15–16).

Loving God, we are watermarked by baptism. You are indelibly within us. Give us strength to do as we should when we are too weak on our own. Grant us wakefulness to your love as we await the coming of Jesus. Amen.

Invite the persons at the table to tell stories from their life about a time when they glimpsed God through the poor, the marginalized, or the ordinary.

Pray the prayer every evening this week as the first, second, and third candles are lit for the evening meal.

THE FOURTH SUNDAY OF ADVENT: THE JESSE TREE AND THE GIVING TREE

Another common Christian symbol during Advent is the Jesse Tree. This tree represents the genealogy of Christ, showing the generations of Jesus back to Adam as was written in the Gospel of Matthew. Across time the custom in many parishes or congregations was to hang the names of people in the community on a living tree at Christmas time. That practice developed into a common modern tradition called the Giving Tree. Individual parishes or congregations set up a tree in the church during Advent on which are the names, ages, and genders of children or adults who are in special need. Members of the community can take a name from the tree and purchase a gift for that individual on behalf of the faith community.

If your parish or congregation has a Giving Tree that you participate in, hang the tag on your own Christmas tree as a reminder of your concern for this individual. Or, if not, make tags for the tree with the names of your own family and friends as a special reminder of the blessings they bring to your life. This fourth week of Advent look for a way you can assist someone in need.

Activity

Place the figures of St. Joseph and the Virgin Mary in the crèche. Imagine the hardships of a young family about to give birth in such a place: Joseph, a poor man in a peculiar situation with a pregnant wife, and Mary, a girl about to have her first child amongst the animals. Let their presence be a reminder of the sacrifice of their faith, and of the bounty that you enjoy. Save the Christ child until Christmas Eve and then place it in the crib with thanks and joy.

During the evening meal on the fourth Sunday of Advent light the first, second, third and fourth Advent candles. Read the following Scripture and pray the Advent prayer.

And blessed is she who believed that there would be fulfillment of what was spoken to her by the Lord (Lk 1:45).

Holy, helping, healing God, you watched over Joseph and Mary as they waited in the manger for the fulfillment of your promise. As we wait protect us with your love that we may grow in faithfulness and desire to do your will. Amen.

Invite the persons at the table to tell stories of a time when they were afraid or vulnerable and yet felt the presence of God, fulfilling God's promise to be with us always.

Pray the prayer every evening this week as all four candles are lit for the evening meal.

PART SIX

Additional Resources

READING CYCLE FOR ADVENT AND CHRISTMAS

Advent Daily Catholic Lectionary Cycle

This is the maximum number of readings available for Advent when the first Sunday is November 27 and there are 28 days in the season. Advent can start as late as December 3 and have as few as 21 days. See note 2 for the order of readings in shorter Advent seasons.

DAY OF THE WEEK	DATE	READINGS
1st Sunday of Advent	11/27	Depends on Year (A, B, or C)
Monday[1]	28	Isaiah 2:1–5; Psalm 122:1–9; Matthew 8:5–11
Tuesday	29	Isaiah 11:1–10; Psalm 72:1, 7–8, 12–13, 17; Luke 10:21–24
Wednesday	30	Isaiah 25:6–10; Psalm 23:1–6; Matthew 15:29–37
Thursday	12/1	Isaiah 26:1–6; Psalm 118:1, 8–9, 19–21, 25–27; Matthew 7:21, 24–27
Friday	2	Isaiah 29:17–24; Psalm 27:1, 4, 13–14; Matthew 9:27–31
Saturday	3	Isaiah 30:19–21, 23–26; Psalm 147:1–6; Matthew 9:35–10:1, 6–8
2nd Sunday of Advent	4	Depends on Year (A, B, or C)

DAY OF THE WEEK	DATE	READINGS
Monday	5	Isaiah 35:1–10; Psalm 85:9–14; Luke 5:17–26
Tuesday	6	Isaiah 40:1–11; Psalm 96:1–3, 10–13; Matthew 18:12–14
Wednesday	7	Isaiah 40:25–31; Psalm 103:1–4, 8, 10; Matthew 11:28–30
Thursday	8	Isaiah 41:13–20; Psalm 145:1, 9–13; Matthew 11:11–15
Friday	9	Isaiah 48:17–19; Psalm 1:1–4, 6; Matthew 11:16–19
Saturday	10	Sirach 48:1–4, 9–11; Psalm 80:2–3, 15–19; Matthew 17:10–13
3rd Sunday of Advent	11	Depends on Year (A, B, or C)
Monday	12	Numbers 24:2–7, 15–17; Psalm 25:4–9; Matthew 21:23–27
Tuesday	13	Zephaniah 3:1–2, 9–13; Psalm 34:2–3, 6–19, 23; Matthew 21:28–32
Wednesday	14	Isaiah 45:6–8, 18, 21–25; Psalm 85:9–14; Luke 7:18–23
Thursday	15	Isaiah 54:1–10; Psalm 30:2, 4–6, 11–13; Luke 7:24–30
Friday	16	Isaiah 56:1–3, 6–8; Psalm 67:2–3, 5, 7–8; John 5:33–36
Saturday[2]	17	Genesis 49:2, 8–10; Psalm 72:3–4, 7–8, 17; Matthew 1:1–17
4th Sunday of Advent	18	Depends on Year (A, B, or C)

DAY OF THE WEEK	DATE	READINGS
If 18th is a weekday:		Jeremiah 23:5–8; Psalm 72:1, 12–13, 18–19; Matthew 1:18–24
Monday	19	Judges 13:2–7, 24–25a; Psalm 71:3–6, 16–17; Luke 1:5–25
Tuesday	20	Isaiah 7:10–14; Psalm 24:1–6; Luke 1:26–38
Wednesday	21	Songs 2:8–14 OR Zephaniah 3:14–18; Psalm 33:2–3, 11–12, 20–21; Luke 1:39–45
Thursday	22	1 Samuel 1:24–28; 1 Samuel 2:1, 4–8; Luke 1:46–56
Friday	23	Malachi 3:1–4, 23–24; Psalm 25:4–5, 8–10, 14; Luke 1:57–66
Saturday	24	2 Samuel 7:1–5, 8–11, 16; Psalm 89:2–7, 27, 29; Luke 1:67–79
Sunday	25	Christmas

Notes:

1. If it is Year A for the Sunday readings, this OT reading changes to Isaiah 4:2–6.

2. Beginning December 17 the readings are calendar specific up to the December 24. Readings read between Monday to Friday of the third week of Advent will be superceded depending upon what day of the week December 17 falls. However, Sunday readings always take precedence over readings for December 17–24 when one of those days is a Sunday.

Annual Reading Cycle [1]

Catholic Lectionary	Revised Common Lectionary
Year A:	Year A:
2002	2002
2005	2005
2008	2008
2011	2011
Year B:	Year B:
2003	2003
2006	2006
2009	2009
2012	2012
Year C:	Year C:
2004	2004
2007	2007
2010	2010
2013	2013

Note:

1. The liturgical year begins on the First Sunday of Advent in the preceding calendar year. Thus, Liturgical Year 2005 begins on November 28, 2004 the First Sunday of Advent. The Liturgical Year 2006 begins on November 27, 2005.

Advent Readings for Sundays, Years A, B, and C

CATHOLIC LECTIONARY

Sunday	Year A	Year B	Year C
1st Sunday	Isaiah 2:1–5 Psalm 122:1–9 Romans 13:11–14a Matthew 24:37–44	Isaiah 63:16b–17, 19b, 64:2–7 Psalm 80:2–3, 15–19 1 Corinthians 1:3–9 Mark 13:33–37	Jeremiah 33:14–16 Psalm 25:4–5, 8–10, 14 1 Thess. 3:12–4:2 Luke 21:25–28, 34–36
2nd Sunday	Isaiah 11:1–10 Psalm 72:1–2, 7–8, 12–13, 17 Romans 15:4–9 Matthew 3:1–12	Isaiah 40:1–5, 9–11 Psalm 85:9–14 2 Peter 3:8–14 Mark 1:1–8	Baruch 5:1–9 Psalm 126:1–6 Philippians 1:4–6, 8–11 Luke 3:1–6
3rd Sunday	Isaiah 35:1–6, 10 Psalm 146:6–10 James 5:7–10 Matthew 11:2–11	Isaiah 61:1–2, 10–11 Luke 1:46–50, 53–54 1 Thess. 5:16–24 John 1:6–8, 19–28	Zephaniah 3:14–18 Isaiah 12:2–6 Philippians 4:4–7 Luke 3:10–18
4th Sunday	Isaiah 7:10–14 Psalm 24:1–6 Romans 1:1–7 Matthew 1:18–24	2 Samuel 7:1–5, 8b–12, 16 Psalm 89:2–5, 27, 29 Romans 16:25–27 Luke 1:26–38	Micah 5:1–4 Psalm 80:2–3, 15–16 Hebrews 10:5–10 Luke 1:39–45

REVISED COMMON LECTIONARY

Sunday	Year A	Year B	Year C
1st Sunday	Isaiah 2:1–5 Psalm 122 Romans 13:11–14 Matthew 24:36–44	Isaiah 64:1–9 Psalm 80:1–7, 17–19 1 Corinthians 1:3–9 Mark 13:24–37	Jeremiah 33:14–16 Psalm 25:1–10 1 Thess. 3:9–13 Luke 21:25–36
2nd Sunday	Isaiah 11:1–10 Psalm 72:1–7, 18–19 Romans 15:4–13 Matthew 3:1–12	Isaiah 40:1–11 Psalm 85:1–2, 8–13 2 Peter 3:8–15a Mark 1:1–8	Malachi 3:1–4 Luke 1:68–79 Philippians 1:3–11 Luke 3:1–6
3rd Sunday	Isaiah 35:1–10 Psalm 146:5–10 James 5:7–10 Matthew 11:2–11	Isaiah 61:1–4, 8–11 Psalm 126 1 Thessalonians 5:16–24 John 1:6–8, 19–28	Zephaniah 3:14–20 Isaiah 12:2–6 Philippians 4:4–7 Luke 3:7–18
4th Sunday	Isaiah 7:10–16 Psalm 80:1–7, 17–19 Romans 1:1–7 Matthew 1:18–25	2 Samuel 7:1–11, 16 Psalm 126 Romans 16:25–27 Luke 1:26–38	Micah 5:2–5a Psalm 80:1–7 Hebrews 10:5–10 Luke 1:39–45

Christmas Reading Cycle

CATHOLIC LECTIONARY

DAY	DATE	READINGS
Christmas	12/25	*Vigil:* Isaiah 62:1–5; Psalm 89:4–5, 16–17, 27, 29; Acts 13:16–17, 22–25; Matthew 1:1–25
		Midnight: Isaiah 9:1–6; Psalm 96:1–3, 11–13; Titus 2:11–14; Luke 2:1–14
		Dawn: Isaiah 62:11–12; Psalm 97:1, 6, 11–12; Titus 3:4–7; Luke 2:15–20
		Day: Isaiah 52:7–10; Psalm 98:1–6; Hebrews 1:1–6; John 1:1–18
Memorial of St. Stephen, First Martyr	12/26	Acts 6:8–10, 7:54–59; Psalm 31:3–8, 17, 21; Matthew 10:17–22
Feast of St. John, Apostle, Evangelist	12/27	1 John 1:1–4; Psalm 96:1–2, 5–6, 11–12; John 20:2–8
Feast of the Holy Innocents	12/28	1 John 1:5–2:2; Psalm 124:2–8; Matthew 2:13–18;
5th Day in the Octave of Christmas	12/29	1 John 2:3–11; Psalm 96:1–6; Luke 2:22–35
6th Day in the Octave of Christmas	12/30	1 John 2:12–17; Psalm 96:7–10; Luke 2:36–40
7th Day in the Octave of Christmas	12/31	1 John 2:18–21; Psalm 96:1–2, 11–13; John 1:1–18;

DAY	DATE	READINGS
Solemnity of the Blessed Virgin Mary, Mother of God	1/1	Numbers 6:22–27; Psalm 67:2–8; Galatians 4:4–7; Luke 2:16–21
Christmas Weekday	1/ 2	1 John 2:22–28; Psalm 98:1–4; John 1:19–28
Christmas Weekday	1/3	1 John 2:29–3:6; Psalm 98:1, 3–6; John 1:29–34
Christmas Weekday	1/ 4	1 John 3:7–10; Psalm 98:1, 7–9; John 1:35–42;
Christmas Weekday	1/5	1 John 3:11–21; Psalm 100:1–5; John 1:43–51
Christmas Weekday	1/6[1]	1 John 5:5–13; Psalm 147:12–15, 19–20 Mark 1:7–11
First Sunday after Christmas Day, Feast of the Holy Family[2]		Sirach 3:2–6, 12–14; Psalm 128:1–5; Colossians 3:12–21; Year A: Matthew 2:13–15, 19–23 Year B: Luke 2:22–40 Year C: Luke 2:41–52
Solemnity of the Epiphany of the Lord[3]		Isaiah 60:1–6; Psalm 72:1–2, 7–8, 10–13; Ephesians 3:2–3, 5–6; Matthew 2:1–12

Notes

1. This is the reading for January 6 when Epiphany is celebrated on the second Sunday after Christmas Day and January 6 falls prior to Epiphany.

2.This reading substitutes any other day in January that falls on the first Sunday after Christmas.

3.This is the Epiphany reading regardless of whether it is celebrated on January 6 or on the second Sunday after Christmas.

REVISED COMMON LECTIONARY

DAY	DATE	READINGS
Nativity of the Lord, Proper I	12/25	Isaiah 9:2–7; Psalm 96; Titus 2:11–14; Luke 2:1–14
Nativity of the Lord, Proper II	12/25	Isaiah 62:6–12; Psalm 97; Titus 3:4–7; Luke 2:8–20
Nativity of the Lord, Proper III	12/25	Isaiah 52:7–10; Psalm 98; Hebrews 1:1–4; John 1:1–14
1st Sunday after Christmas	Varies	Isaiah 63:7–9; Psalm 148; Hebrews 2:10–18; Matthew 2:13–23
Holy Name of Jesus (Mary Mother of God)	1/1	Numbers 6:22–27; Psalm 8; Galatians 4:4–7; Luke 2:15–21
New Year's Day	1/1	Ecclesiastes 3:1–13; Psalm 8; Revelation 21:1–6a; Matthew 25:31–46
2nd Sunday after Christmas (if falls before Epiphany)	Varies	Jeremiah 31:7–14; Psalm 147:12–20; Ephesians 1:3–14; John 1:10–18
Epiphany of the Lord	Varies	Isaiah 60:1–6; Psalm 72:1–7, 10–14; Ephesians 3:1–12; Matthew 2:1–2

Bibliography

Bibles

The Holy Bible: Containing the Old and New Testaments, New Revised Standard Version. World Bible Publishers, Inc., 1989.

The New Oxford Annotated NRSV Bible with Apocrypha. Oxford University Press, 2001.

Lectionary Resources

Archdiocese of Chicago, *Liturgy and Appointment Calendar 2003.* Chicago: Liturgy Training Publications, 2002.

The National Conference of Catholic Bishops and confirmed by the Apostolic See, *The Roman Missal: Lectionary for Mass.* Catholic Book Publishing Co., 1970.

Other Resources

Adam, Adolf, *Foundations of Liturgy: An Introduction to Its History and Practice.* Collegeville, Minn.: Liturgical Press, 1992.

Boswell, John, *Same Sex Unions in Pre-Modern Europe.* New York: Random House, Inc., 1994.

Broderick, Robert C., ed., *The Catholic Encyclopedia.* Thomas Nelson Publishers, 1987.

England, Michael, *The Bible and Homosexuality.* Gaithersburg, Maryland: The Chi Rho Press, Inc., 1998.

The Essential Advent and Christmas Handbook: A Daily Companion With a Glossary of Key Terms. Liguori, Minn.: Redemptorist Pastoral Publications, 2000.

Jung, Patricia Beattie, with Joseph Andrew Coray, eds., *Sexual Diversity and Catholicism*. Collegeville, Minn.: The Liturgical Press, 2001.

Meisel, Anthony C., and M. L. del Mastro, translators, *The Rule of St. Benedict*. Garden City, New York: Doubleday & Co., Inc., 1975.

Worship Resources

Board of Publication, Lutheran Church in America, *Lutheran Book of Worship*. Minneapolis, Minn.: Augsburg Publishing House, 1978.

The Divine Office revised by decree of the Second Vatican Ecumenical Council and published by authority of Pope Paul VI, *Christian Prayer: The Liturgy of the Hours*. Boston, Mass.: Daughters of St. Paul, 1976.

Finnerty, D. Joseph and George J. Ryan, *Morning and Evening Prayer: Selections from The Liturgy of the Hours*. New York: Regina Press, 1973.

Lefebvre, Dom Gaspar, O.S.B., *Saint Andrew Daily Missal*. St. Paul, Minn.: The E.M. Lohmon Co., 1940.

BOOK NOTES—FOR ANOTHER FLOCK
Related Titles from The Pilgrim Press

COMING OUT THROUGH FIRE
Surviving the Trauma of Homophobia
LEANNE MCCALL TIGERT AND TIMOTHY BROWN, EDS.

A book for lesbians, gays, bisexuals, and transgendered persons seeking to move through the trauma of homophobia with the passion and power of transformation. Also useful for pastors, therapists, and other counseling professionals who seek to confront prejudice and fear and further the process of healing and recovery in the church and the wider community.　ISBN 0-8298-1293-8

Paper, 148 pages, **$13.00**

COMING OUT TO PARENTS
A Two-Way Survival Guide for Lesbians and Gay Men and Their Parents
MARY V. BORHEK

For lesbian and gay individuals, this book explores the fears and misgivings accompanying their revelation to their parents, and offers suggestions on how and when to come out, what reactions to expect, and how to deal with ensuing awkwardness. It guides parents through natural feelings of grief and loss and shows how understanding, compassion, and insight can lead to deeper love and acceptance.　ISBN 0-8298-0957-0

Paper, 310 pages, **$16.00**

COMING OUT WHILE STAYING IN
Struggles and Celebrations of Lesbians, Gays, and Bisexuals in the Church
LEANNE MCCALL TIGERT

Tigert reflects upon her own personal struggle with the church as a source of pain, alienation, support, and spiritual renewal, and shares others' struggles with the church in the hope of opening the doors to change, healing, and liberation for LGBT individuals.　ISBN 0-8298-1150-8

Paper, 182 pages, **$15.00**

COMING OUT YOUNG AND FAITHFUL

LEANNE MCCALL TIGERT AND TIMOTHY BROWN, EDS.

This groundbreaking collection comes from lesbian, gay, bisexual, transgender, and questioning teens who share their experiences in their communities and churches. Includes resources for ministry and advocacy to help open the doors of affirmation, love, and commitment to the needs of LGBT youth and young adults.   ISBN 0-8298-1414-0

Paper, 112 pages, **$13.00**

COURAGE TO LOVE

Liturgies for the Lesbian, Gay, Bisexual, and Transgender Community

GEOFFREY DUNCAN, ED.

Winner of a 2002 Lambda Literary Award for Religion/Spirituality. An exceptional collection of worship and other liturgical resources inclusive of and sensitive to the LGBT community for both clergy and lay people. Beneficial for relationships with families, church, and community. Includes liturgies for the Eucharist and same-sex marriages.   ISBN 0-8298-1468-X

Paper, 384 pages, **$23.00**

THE ESSENTIAL GAY MYSTICS

ANDREW HARVEY, ED.

From Sappho to Whitman, Vergil to Audre Lorde, *The Essential Gay Mystics* is a collection of mystical writings covering the period from early Greek writers to the 20th century. Contains over 60 selections celebrating those who love others of the same sex.   ISBN 0-8298-1443-4

Paper, 304 pages, **$18.00**

GAY THEOLOGY WITHOUT APOLOGY

GARY DAVID COMSTOCK

A case for the acknowledgement of varied expressions of humanity. Comstock presents essays that express a specific gay theology, which is an understanding of his personal concern[em dash]for all people to recognize that there is a true benefit to fully appreciating gayness as a part of being both human and Christian.

ISBN 0-8298-0944-9

Paper, 184 pages, **$16.00**

MY SON ERIC

A Mother Struggles to Accept Her Gay Son and Discovers Herself
Revised and Expanded

MARY V. BORHEK

A revised and expanded edition of an American classic from 1979, *My Son Eric* sounds the trumpet for love and acceptance of gays and lesbians. Borhek has spent over 20 years at the center of many advancements in gay and lesbian life in the U.S.   ISBN 0-8298-1427-2

Paper, 176 pages,$14.00

OUR DAUGHTER MARTHA

A Family Struggles with Coming Out
MARCY CLEMENTS HENRIKSON

Combining her experience with excerpts from her daughter's journal, author and laywoman Henrikson takes us on her journey to accepting her lesbian daughter as well as her active role in support of lesbian and gay rights in the church and society. Ideal for families and congregations with gay and lesbian members.   ISBN 0-8298-1432-9

Paper, 112 pages, $10.00

OUT ON HOLY GROUND

Meditations on Gay Men's Spirituality
DONALD L. BOISVERT

Boisvert presents his own meditations through the context of theology, myths, rituals, symbols, and spiritual culture in order to create a compelling portrait of gay spirituality as a serious yet perceptive and provocative cultural expression in North America.   ISBN 0-8298-1369-1

Paper, 148 pages, $20.00

RECONCILING JOURNEY

A Devotional Workbook for Lesbian and Gay Christians

MICHAL ANNE PEPPER

An interactive, nine-week spiritual resource for lesbian and gay Christians who find themselves facing issues regarding their sexuality and their spirituality. Each day includes a scripture passage and journaling space to make notes and/or write prayers about that day's topic. Can be used in an individual or group setting. ISBN 0-8298-1569-4

Paper w/French flaps, 128 pages, **$20.00**

SANCTITY AND MALE DESIRE

A Gay Reading of Saints

DONALD L. BOISVERT

An evocative look at how saints—and one's devotion to them—can be sites for the confirmation and celebration of homoerotic desire. The book contains twelve chapters that focus on saints, including: Michael the Archangel; Sebastian and Tarcisius; John the Baptist; Joseph; Paul and Augustine; the Ugandan and North American martyrs; Francis of Assisi; Dominic Savio; Damien; Peter Julian Eymard, and more. ISBN 0-8298-1523-6

Paper, 224 pages, **$22.00**

To order these or any other books from The Pilgrim Press, call or write to:

The Pilgrim Press
700 Prospect Avenue
Cleveland, OH 44115-1100

Phone orders: 800.537.3394 (M–F, 8:30am-4:30pm ET)
Fax orders: 216.736.2206

Please include shipping charges of $5.00 for the first book and 75¢ for each additional book.

Or order from our web site at www.thepilgrimpress.com.

Prices subject to change without notice.